Essential Dewey

Essential Dewey

J. H. Bowman

NEAL-SCHUMAN PUBLISHERS, INC.
NEW YORK

Published by Neal Schuman Publishers, Inc.
100 William Street, Suite 2004
New York, NY 10038

First published in the UK by Facet Publishing (wholly owned by CILIP: the Chartered Institute of Library and Information Professionals), 2005. This US edition 2005.

The paper used in this publication meets the minimum requirements of American National Standard for Information Sciences–Permanence of Paper for Printed Library Materials, ANSI Z39.48–1992.

ISBN 1-55570-544-8

Printed and made in the United Kingdom.

Contents

Preface

This book is intended as an introduction to the Dewey Decimal Classification, edition 22. It is not a substitute for it, and I assume that you have it, all four volumes of it, by you while reading the book.

I have deliberately included only a short section on WebDewey. This is partly because WebDewey is likely to change more frequently than the printed version, but also because this book is intended to help you use the scheme regardless of the manifestation in which it appears. If you have a subscription to WebDewey and not the printed volumes you may be able to manage with that, but you may then find my references to volumes and page numbers baffling.

All the examples and exercises are real; what is not real is the idea that you can classify something without seeing more than the title. However, there is nothing that I can do about this, and I have therefore tried to choose examples whose titles adequately express their subject-matter. Sometimes when you look at the 'answers' you may feel that you have been cheated, but I hope that this will be seldom.

Two people deserve special thanks. My colleague Vanda Broughton has read drafts of the book and made many suggestions. Ross Trotter, chair of the CILIP Dewey Decimal Classification Committee, who knows more about Dewey than anyone in Britain today, has commented extensively on it and as far as possible has saved me from error, as well as suggesting many improvements. What errors remain are due to me alone.

Thanks are also owed to OCLC Online Computer Library Center, for permission to reproduce some specimen pages of DDC 22. Excerpts from the Dewey Decimal Classification are taken from the Dewey Decimal Classification and Relative Index, Edition 22 which is Copyright 2003 OCLC Online Computer Library Center, Inc. DDC, Dewey, Dewey Decimal Classification and WebDewey are registered trademarks of OCLC Online Computer Library Center, Inc.

J. H. B.

1 Introduction and background

Purpose of classification

In this book we are learning about one particular library classification, but before doing that we need to consider classification in general. We associate classification particularly with libraries, but in fact many things that we do involve classification. When we go shopping we have to decide which shop to go into, because shops generally deal only with certain *kinds of goods*. When we get inside we have to find the right part of the shop, and in most cases goods which are similar are grouped together. In a supermarket we expect to find butter near to cheese because they are both dairy products. We may or may not also find milk nearby; if we do not, it is because milk may require a different kind of storage and display.

This may seem a trivial example, but in fact it illustrates a perennial problem with classification of all kinds. Classification is essentially just grouping, putting like with like, but there is usually more than one way of classifying things. For example, we usually find that frozen fish is in a different place from fresh fish because it needs different storage conditions, and in this case the nature of the storage takes precedence over the nature of the goods.

It is just the same in libraries. Library classification has two main purposes:

- to put similar items together, thereby also separating them from different subjects
- to arrange the subjects generally in some kind of rational order.

Each of these presents difficulties. I do not propose to discuss the second purpose at all in this book; it has been a much debated subject, and different classification schemes have arrived at different orders for the main subjects. The main class order in Dewey may not be ideal, but it is the way it is, and there is no likelihood that it will ever be changed, which means that we just have to accept it.

Going back to the first purpose, there are usually several ways of determining what is 'similar'. Many libraries make a fundamental division by physical form, so that, for example, videos are shelved separately from books; others try to integrate all formats into a single sequence based on subject. For physical convenience most libraries separate particularly large books from the ordinary size and put them in a different sequence. Ready reference books are also usually put in a separate section.

Citation order

Physical form of this kind is easy enough to understand, and it does not normally enter into the structure of the classification scheme; it is more usual to use prefixes like Q or OVERSIZE or REF, for example, rather than have special numbers. But in other respects the question of different aspects of a subject can be a major difficulty. How do you decide which has priority? Suppose, for example, that you have a book about education in London. Do you put it with other items on education or with other items on London? This is a matter of what is called *citation* order, which really just means *which aspect of a compound subject do you give priority to?*

The standard policy in most classification schemes is that in cases where one of the aspects of the subject is geographic this is considered to be less important, and this is certainly the way in which Dewey would treat such an item. But you might have a special collection of London material, in which case some other arrangement might be desirable and you might want to give priority to London. With a few exceptions, Dewey does not generally allow this kind of variation or choice; you have to do what the instructions say.

Relative location

A classification scheme usually achieves a third purpose, which I did not mention earlier: it provides a means for a library user to look up a specific item in the catalogue and then go to find it on the shelves. This is rather different from the other purposes, in that it could be achieved without using classification at all. You could just number all the items in order of acquisition and shelve them in the same order. The user would be able to find the number from the catalogue and retrieve the item.

If the users of the library have no direct access to the shelves, but have to request each item from a catalogue, the actual shelf arrangement does not much matter, and it is possible simply to number the items in stock and to shelve them in that order. In public libraries systematic classification really only came into use when access to the shelves began to be provided in the last decade of the nineteenth century. In other kinds of library, even when open access was provided, the classification was usually very broad, and consisted chiefly of numbered bays, then numbered shelves within the bay, and numbered books on the shelf. When a section was full, it was necessary to renumber all the books if they had to be moved round.

The great benefit of Dewey's scheme when it was first devised was that the books are numbered *relative to each other*, rather than relative to the fixed shelves. For this reason it is known as a *relative location* system. All modern classification schemes are relative location.

Regardless of the physical arrangement of the stock, the users of a library can be helped by a classification scheme if a classified catalogue is produced. This allows them to browse by subject, and to find related subjects together in a way which does not happen in alphabetical subject catalogues. Classification schemes can also be useful in arranging browsable lists of web resources.

History of the Dewey Decimal Classification

Melvil Dewey first published his *A classification and subject index for cataloguing and arranging the books and pamphlets of a library* in 1876 (Dewey, 1876), after using the scheme for three years in his own library, Amherst College, Massachusetts. The first edition had only 44 pages and provided numbers from 0 to 999, though at least a hundred of these were not used; there were no decimal places. In later editions decimals were introduced, and the numbers below 100 were extended to three digits (001 rather than 1, and 020 rather than 20, etc.). Since then no class-number has ever been shorter than three digits. A great deal has been written about Dewey and his classification, and there is no need for me to repeat it here. (For a detailed history of the scheme up to the 18th edition see Comaromi, 1976; for a good modern biography of Dewey himself see Wiegand, 1996.)

Dewey was closely involved in the revision of the scheme until his death in 1930. He had established his own publishing house, the Forest Press, to carry on the scheme, and in 1988 this was taken over by OCLC Online Computer Center, Inc., which is now responsible for it. The number of volumes has increased, reaching four with Edition 20, and the latest edition, Edition 22, was published in 2003.

To save space I shall refer to the scheme as Dewey throughout, and this means Edition 22, or DDC 22.

The abridged edition

As well as the full edition, there has been a series of abridged editions, which are designed for libraries that do not wish to use the detail of the full scheme. Because there have not been as many abridged editions as there have of the full, their edition numbers do not correspond, which can be rather confusing. The abridged edition corresponding with the full Edition 22 is number 14.

In Britain the School Library Association publishes a very much simplified version under licence from OCLC, called *Primary school classification scheme*. This is intended to cover subjects included in the National Curriculum.

How the scheme is revised

Revision is under the direction of an Editorial Policy Committee, which includes representatives from a number of countries (but mainly the United States). In the United Kingdom CILIP has a Dewey Decimal Classification Committee which includes representatives from a variety of libraries, and one of its members is the British representative on the Editorial Policy Committee. The practical work of redrafting is largely in the hands of the Editor and a small number of assistant editors.

In the United States the Library of Congress has a special department, the Decimal Classification Division, which allocates Dewey numbers to much of the material received in the Library. This is done purely for the benefit of other libraries which may obtain their catalogue records via the Library of Congress; internally the Library uses its own classification scheme.

The editors of Dewey are helped in their work by the staff of the Decimal Classification Division, which is where most of the assistant editors are actually based. Because of this close proximity, the editors are made aware of the type of material which is passing through, and of any changes to the scheme which might therefore be desirable as new subjects come along.

A new printed edition is issued about every seven years, but in the interim minor amendments are posted on the website at: www.oclc.org/ dewey/updates/new/.

Literary warrant

A very important aspect of DDC has always been what is known as *literary warrant*, which in essence means that the provision of numbers in the scheme is based on the existence of works about those subjects. Because of the close connection with the Library of Congress it has often been felt that there is a considerable bias in favour of books, and that other kinds of publication are not so well covered, and this has undoubtedly been true in the past. With the involvement of OCLC in internet cataloguing, however, it is likely to be less of a problem in the future.

A problem with the idea of literary warrant is that subjects go out of fashion, and the treatment of subjects changes. The editors seem to take the view that if little is being published on a subject it is less important to maintain that number in the scheme, even though books already exist on it. This idea has always seemed to me to be misguided, because the older books do not just cease to exist, and they still need to be classified. It seems to be a particular problem with geographical numbers in places like Great Britain, where there have been several reorganizations of local government boundaries. Regrettably, the editors take the view that the provision of numbers in the classification must always be exactly aligned with the latest local government areas. A county like Herefordshire, for example, which is now a unitary authority, has lost the subdivisions which used to exist for individual areas within it.

Sometimes literary warrant seems not to go far enough. For example, some subjects are often dealt with in combination, e.g. Greek and Latin literature. Despite the existence of plenty of books on this combination, there was originally no number for it because logically Greek literature and Latin literature are separate subjects, and it has had to be forced in rather artificially (see p. 120). In this respect the Library of Congress scheme is better adapted to what is actually published.

Shortcomings of the scheme

No one would pretend that the scheme is ideal. There are many unsatisfactory aspects of it, and the editors are gradually trying to put some of them right, but there is a limit to what can be done without causing wholesale reclassification of existing collections. This is so expensive that it is not something that many librarians want to contemplate. A balance has to be struck between improving the scheme and inconveniencing those who use existing collections.

Some of the principal complaints are as follows:

- Because of the 'disciplinary' nature of the scheme, more subjects are 'scattered' than need to be.
- Because the scheme is now very old and has grown in a very haphazard way, some sections are much more detailed than others.
- There is an unbalanced use of the notation, because of the arbitrary division of knowledge into ten main classes.
- Some subjects that would be better together are separated, notably 400 Language and 800 Literature.
- The scheme is unduly prescriptive: there are many rules, and unless you read the instructions very carefully you are likely to break them (you may of course not care about this).
- The scheme does not cope well with items that cover multiple subjects, and it is often difficult to show relationships between subjects.
- The scheme shows a rather 19th-century White Anglo-Saxon Protestant world-view, and is not sufficiently responsive to the needs of other cultures; this problem is to some extent being addressed by the editors as far as possible within the existing structure.

The future

Despite all the disadvantages, it is likely that the use of Dewey will continue to increase. Other schemes perhaps have advantages over Dewey: the Bliss Bibliographic Classification (2nd edition), for example, is based on much sounder theory and is generally much more suitable for non-American libraries. In the United States some libraries have reclassified to Library of Congress in order to take advantage of the class-numbers appearing in their records, but on the whole the labour involved in reclassifying a large library is so great that only very few will undertake it. It therefore seems likely that Dewey will continue to be used for the foreseeable future, perhaps as long as libraries or collections of information exist, and that its use will continue to spread.

The scheme has been translated into over 30 languages, and this number also continues to increase.

2 Outline of the scheme

Physical arrangement

Dewey has grown very much since the first edition, and now occupies four volumes. Their content is divided as follows:

1 Introduction
  Manual
  Tables
  Lists of changes from the previous edition
2–3 The schedules themselves
4 Relative index

This brings us immediately to an important point in which Dewey terminology differs from that of some other schemes. The *schedules* are the main part of the scheme, where all the numbers for the subjects are to be found (000–999); the *tables* consist of tables of *additional* numbers, which may in some circumstances be added at the end of numbers obtained from the schedules.

The Introduction is written by the editors of the scheme. It not only tells you how to use Dewey but also gives useful information about the nature of bibliographic classification in general.

The Manual gives further guidance on using the scheme, mainly on the more difficult aspects, and information which would take up too much space if it were included in the schedules. In recent years there has been a policy of including as much as possible in the schedules, because otherwise it is easy to miss it. You should have a good look through the Manual so as to get an idea of what it contains.

➤ Always look out for instructions in the schedules referring you to the Manual.

The general nature of the scheme

You probably already know that the scheme is based on the principle of dividing all knowledge into ten great divisions, numbered from 0 to 9; this is the reason why it is called decimal. These ten divisions are usually referred to in Dewey as 'main classes', and are:

000 Computer science, information and general works
100 Philosophy and psychology
200 Religion
300 Social sciences
400 Language
500 Science
600 Technology
700 Arts and recreation
800 Literature
900 History and geography

Notice that because no number can have fewer than three digits these ten divisions are presented as 000, 100, 200, etc., to 900; the 0s are used simply as 'fillers', to make up the required number of digits.

➤ A zero in Dewey never *means* anything in itself; it is used either as a filler like this or to keep other groups of digits apart. We shall see this again many times.

Hierarchy

Division of the ten main classes continues on the same principle, e.g.

510
    511
    512
    513, etc.
520
530, etc.

In each case nine subdivisions are available. Figure 2.1 (opposite) shows the 'hundred divisions', i.e. all the numbers ending in 0. Generally the notation is *expressive*, which means that it is used in a way which expresses this hierarchical aspect of the scheme, so that the further down the hierarchy of subject divisions you go the more digits are added to the numbers. This means that if 500 denotes Science any number starting with a 5 *must* in some way be

Second Summary
The Hundred Divisions

000   **Computer science, knowledge & systems**
010   Bibliographies
020   Library & information sciences
030   Encyclopedias & books of facts
040   [Unassigned]
050   Magazines, journals & serials
060   Associations, organizations & museums
070   News media, journalism & publishing
080   Quotations
090   Manuscripts & rare books

100   **Philosophy**
110   Metaphysics
120   Epistemology
130   Parapsychology & occultism
140   Philosophical schools of thought
150   Psychology
160   Logic
170   Ethics
180   Ancient, medieval & eastern philosophy
190   Modern western philosophy

200   **Religion**
210   Philosophy & theory of religion
220   The Bible
230   Christianity & Christian theology
240   Christian practice & observance
250   Christian pastoral practice & religious orders
260   Christian organization, social work & worship
270   History of Christianity
280   Christian denominations
290   Other religions

300   **Social sciences, sociology & anthropology**
310   Statistics
320   Political science
330   Economics
340   Law
350   Public administration & military science
360   Social problems & social services
370   Education
380   Commerce, etiquette & folklore
390   Customs, etiquette & folklore

400   **Language**
410   Linguistics
420   English & Old English languages
430   German & related languages
440   French & related languages
450   Italian, Romanian & related languages
460   Spanish & Portuguese languages
470   Latin & Italic languages
480   Classical & modern Greek languages
490   Other languages

500   **Science**
510   Mathematics
520   Astronomy
530   Physics
540   Chemistry
550   Earth sciences & geology
560   Fossils & prehistoric life
570   Life sciences; biology
580   Plants (Botany)
590   Animals (Zoology)

600   **Technology**
610   Medicine & health
620   Engineering
630   Agriculture
640   Home & family management
650   Management & public relations
660   Chemical engineering
670   Manufacturing
680   Manufacture for specific uses
690   Building & construction

700   **Arts**
710   Landscaping & area planning
720   Architecture
730   Sculpture, ceramics & metalwork
740   Drawing & decorative arts
750   Painting
760   Graphic arts
770   Photography & computer art
780   Music
790   Sports, games & entertainment

800   **Literature, rhetoric & criticism**
810   American literature in English
820   English & Old English literatures
830   German & related literatures
840   French & related literatures
850   Italian, Romanian & related literatures
860   Spanish & Portuguese literatures
870   Latin & Italic literatures
880   Classical & modern Greek literatures
890   Other literatures

900   **History**
910   Geography & travel
920   Biography & genealogy
930   History of ancient world (to ca. 499)
940   History of Europe
950   History of Asia
960   History of Africa
970   History of North America
980   History of South America
990   History of other areas

Consult schedules for complete and exact headings

Figure 2.1

part of Science. (Not all schemes use notation in this way; some just move on from one number to another without any regard for hierarchy, because that is irrelevant to them.)

The idea of dividing by ten is obviously very artificial, and has resulted in a rather uneven allocation of numbers. For example, in 100 Philosophy there are still some three-digit numbers which have never been further divided (e.g. each number in the range 160–169, where indeed there are two numbers which are not used at all). On the other hand, in 600 Technology not only is there great and continuous development, but there are also far more topics to be fitted in, and even some quite basic subjects are represented by numbers with several digits. Electrical engineering, for example, is 621.3, and this is greatly subdivided.

Notation

We have already seen that the scheme is decimal. It is entirely numeric, and does not make use of letters in any way, except optionally in a very few places.

➤ No class-number can be shorter than three digits.
➤ If the number is longer than this, it will have the decimal point, or dot, after the third digit. No other punctuation marks are used, and only one decimal point can appear in a class-number. A three-digit number does not have a decimal point.

You will notice when you look at the schedules (or the tables or index) that long numbers are broken down by spaces into groups of three digits. These spaces are put there simply to make the long numbers easier to read. They do not form part of the completed number, and you should close them up when you create your class-number.

Sometimes when looking at catalogue records obtained from external sources you may see the signs / or ' appearing between some digits (in the MARC format a special subfield may be used). These are called segmentation marks, and they indicate places where you can shorten the number if you are using the Abridged edition; they do not form part of the number, and should be omitted.

Also when using external records beware of the fact that sometimes the edition of Dewey is included in a special subfield at the end of the number, as 22 or 21, etc. (Remember too that the older the record the older the edition of Dewey that it will use. You may often have to convert an old number to the edition that you are using in your library.)

Discipline basis

Another important feature of Dewey is that it is what is known as an *aspect classification*, that is, it is based on broad disciplines, rather than on more specific topics. This can be a puzzling concept to understand at first, so let us look at an example.

Think of the subject Animals. What does it mean, without further explanation? You might have something about the biological aspects of animals, or about how to keep animals, as pets or for food, on the worship of animals as gods, on the ethical treatment of animals, on artistic representations of animals, on how to paint pictures of animals, how to take photographs of them, on animals in literature, and many other subjects. In Dewey each of these would go in a different place, and in a different main discipline, because the main discipline is regarded as having priority. For example, it is felt more important to keep all Ethics material together, and then divide it by the subject being treated, and better to keep all Literature together regardless of theme. Under Ethics and under Literature, of course, you can still specify Animals; it is just that they are not given priority in the classification.

A consequence of this discipline basis is that most subjects can be found in more than one place in the scheme, depending on the aspect from which they are treated. This can be irritating, and can sometimes mean that you have to try to make almost impossible distinctions.

A good example is Railways, which has main numbers in Commerce at 385 and in Engineering at 625.1 (not to speak of other more minor aspects elsewhere). Many works deal with all aspects of railways, and, even if they did not, it is still very inconvenient for users to have to look in two widely separated places to find all the material they want. Some libraries therefore decide to put all the material at one place, even if this is not strictly correct in accordance with the scheme.

Another problematic case is City planning, where there are numbers in Sociology and in Civic art. It is very difficult to distinguish these, because most planning has a social purpose, and to have to separate them is unhelpful to users. Even such a specific subject as Skateboards has two numbers.

In most cases, however, one of the numbers provided is used for 'interdisciplinary treatment' of the subject. This can be seen in the relative index, which is explained further in Chapter 3.

Description of the schedules

Let us now have a look at a page of the schedules. Look at Figure 2.2 (opposite), which reproduces p. 481 of Volume 3 of the schedules. At the top of the page you can see a main subject number with its heading:

670 Manufacturing

This is shown in bold, as are all such three-digit subjects.

Subordinate subjects are indicated by decimals. Notice that only the decimal point and the part following it are printed; the main number is not, because it would clutter the page and make the schedules harder to read.

You can always see which main number you are in by looking at the running titles at the top of the page; the number is shown at both the inside and outside edges, with the main subject heading in the middle.

Notes

The heading here illustrates five different kinds of note:

- first there is an 'Including' note
- then there is a 'Class here' note
- next there is a 'Class elsewhere' note
- there is then a brief paragraph of cross-references to other parts of the schedules
- finally there is a note directing you to the Manual.

The purpose of these is largely self-evident. Later (pp. 36–8), we shall see that there is an important difference between an 'Including' note and a 'Class here' note, but for the moment just notice them.

Many headings have no notes at all, of course, and many have one or two kinds, but not all, but their general order will always be as shown here.

Further down the page, you can see that the subheadings

.285 Data processing   Computer applications

and

.42 Factory operations engineering

also show 'Class here' notes.

There is another important aspect of notes to bear in mind: because of the hierarchical nature of the scheme, a note if appropriate can apply to subdivisions further *down* the hierarchy. This is sometimes referred to as 'hierarchical force'.

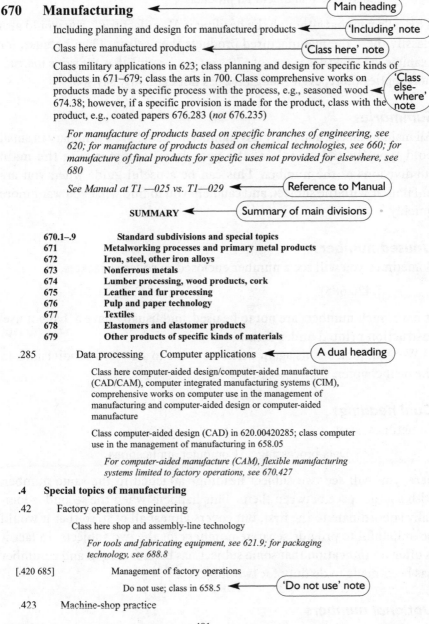

670   Manufacturing   ← Main heading

Including planning and design for manufactured products ← 'Including' note

Class here manufactured products ← 'Class here' note

Class military applications in 623; class planning and design for specific kinds of products in 671–679; class the arts in 700. Class comprehensive works on products made by a specific process with the process, e.g., seasoned wood 674.38; however, if a specific provision is made for the product, class with the product, e.g., coated papers 676.283 (*not* 676.235)   ← 'Class elsewhere' note

For manufacture of products based on specific branches of engineering, see 620; for manufacture of products based on chemical technologies, see 660; for manufacture of final products for specific uses not provided for elsewhere, see 680

See Manual at T1 —025 vs. T1—029 ← Reference to Manual

SUMMARY ← Summary of main divisions

670.1–.9	**Standard subdivisions and special topics**
671	**Metalworking processes and primary metal products**
672	**Iron, steel, other iron alloys**
673	**Nonferrous metals**
674	**Lumber processing, wood products, cork**
675	**Leather and fur processing**
676	**Pulp and paper technology**
677	**Textiles**
678	**Elastomers and elastomer products**
679	**Other products of specific kinds of materials**

.285   Data processing   Computer applications ← A dual heading

Class here computer-aided design/computer-aided manufacture (CAD/CAM), computer integrated manufacturing systems (CIM), comprehensive works on computer use in the management of manufacturing and computer-aided design or computer-aided manufacture

Class computer-aided design (CAD) in 620.00420285; class computer use in the management of manufacturing in 658.05

For computer-aided manufacture (CAM), flexible manufacturing systems limited to factory operations, see 670.427

.4   Special topics of manufacturing

.42   Factory operations engineering

Class here shop and assembly-line technology

For tools and fabricating equipment, see 621.9; for packaging technology, see 688.8

[.420 685]   Management of factory operations

Do not use; class in 658.5 ← 'Do not use' note

.423   Machine-shop practice

481

Figure 2.2

Consider the same example. The second note says

Class here manufactured products

This tells you that although the heading is Manufactur*ing*, you would also classify there the manufactured products themselves. Then because, for example, 677 Textiles is part of 670, you can assume that the same instruction applies there, even though it does not explicitly say so.

Summaries

All main numbers, and many less significant ones, have a summary in small bold type (in the middle of the page here) summarizing the main subdivisions of the number. This can be a useful guide when you are unfamiliar with the subject, and can help you to find what you want more quickly. ·

Unused numbers

Sometimes you will see a number enclosed in square brackets, as

[.420 685]

is here. Such numbers are not to be used, and usually have a 'Do not use' instruction printed under them.

We shall look at this again when we come to standard subdivisions in the next chapter.

Dual headings

Sometimes, as at

.285 Data processing   Computer applications

here, you will see two subject headings attached to the same number, with a large space between them. This happens when the second is logically subordinate to the first, but covers almost all of it, so that it would be unhelpful to provide separate numbers for the two subjects. In fact it is often an indication that some subject has been forced in and a number has been made to do duty for two subjects.

Optional numbers

Not shown in this illustration, but occurring occasionally, are numbers in parentheses (round brackets). These indicate optional numbers, and I shall say more about them later (pp. 69–71).

Centred entries

I have already said that generally the notation is expressive of the hierarchy of division. If we look at the sequence

600   Technology (Applied sciences)
   620   Engineering and allied operations
      621   Applied physics

we can see clearly that each level is subordinate to the one above *and that the notation reflects this* by adding further digits (remember that the zeros are there only to fill out the complete number to three digits).

In certain places something different happens, however. Look at this sequence:

900   Geography, history, and auxiliary disciplines
   970   General history of North America
      973   United States

So far so good; each subordinate level in the subject hierarchy is reflected in the notation, which adds a fresh digit at each stage. But what about individual *parts* of the United States? We should surely expect them to be something like 973.1 to 973.9, to reflect the fact that they are subordinate to 973.

In fact the numbers used for parts of the United States are 974 to 979, which means that the numbers are *the same length* as the number for the United States as a whole. In other words, their appearance does *not* reflect the fact that they represent subordinate concepts, and the notation here is not expressive. Doing this makes shorter numbers, and provides a use for numbers which might otherwise not be used, but it does disrupt the hierarchical appearance of the notation. To draw particular attention to this, wherever it happens, the range of numbers concerned is printed in the middle of the page (hence the term 'centred entry' – 'centered' in American spelling) rather than at the left-hand side, with a > sign against it and a horizontal rule above it.

You might think that this is rather unnecessary, and that the nature of the notation does not matter very much. The main reason why centred entries are always noted so prominently is related to the question of what to do if a work deals with subjects that occur in more than one division of the same class. Because in this situation the notation does *not* reflect the hierarchy of the subject it is essential to have an instruction as to what to do.

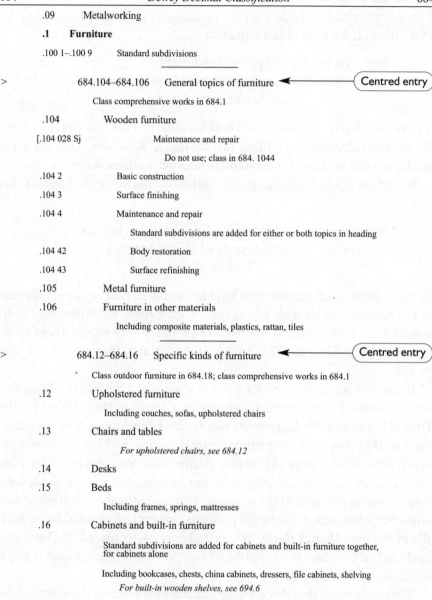

.09   Metalworking

.1   **Furniture**

.100 1–.100 9   Standard subdivisions

>   684.104–684.106   General topics of furniture   ◄——— (Centred entry)

Class comprehensive works in 684.1

.104   Wooden furniture

[.104 028 Sj]   Maintenance and repair

                   Do not use; class in 684. 1044

.104 2   Basic construction

.104 3   Surface finishing

.104 4   Maintenance and repair

                   Standard subdivisions are added for either or both topics in heading

.104 42   Body restoration

.104 43   Surface refinishing

.105   Metal furniture

.106   Furniture in other materials

                   Including composite materials, plastics, rattan, tiles

---

>   684.12–684.16   Specific kinds of furniture   ◄——— (Centred entry)

      *   Class outdoor furniture in 684.18; class comprehensive works in 684.1

.12   Upholstered furniture

                   Including couches, sofas, upholstered chairs

.13   Chairs and tables

                   For upholstered chairs, see 684.12

.14   Desks

.15   Beds

                   Including frames, springs, mattresses

.16   Cabinets and built-in furniture

                   Standard subdivisions are added for cabinets and built-in furniture together, for cabinets alone

                   Including bookcases, chests, china cabinets, dressers, file cabinets, shelving

                   For built-in wooden shelves, see 694.6

Figure 2.3

In the case of parts of the United States we are told to 'Class comprehensive works in 973'.

Figure 2.3 shows two examples of centred entries under 684.1 Furniture. The first centred entry is

> 684.104–684.106 General topics of furniture

This means that each of 684.104, 684.105 and 684.106 and their subdivisions are used for individual topics that apply to furniture.
Likewise, further down the page you can see

> 684.12–684.16 Specific kinds of furniture

In these cases you need to know what to do if you have a work which covers all of the special topics, or all of the specific kinds of furniture. There is therefore always an instruction, as here:

Class comprehensive works in 684.1

➤ The centred entry always shows clearly where the range of numbers using the irregular notation *starts*; it does not so clearly show where it *ends*, and you can only work this out by reading the heading and looking at the range of numbers mentioned.

The tables

All that I have said about the layout of the schedules applies just the same in the tables. The chief difference is that all the numbers in the tables are preceded by a dash — which is simply to show that these numbers cannot be used on their own. They have to be attached to a number from the schedules, and the dash is then omitted.

Figure 2.4 (overleaf) shows the part of Table 2 that covers the Midlands of England. Here you can see some of the changes which have been introduced as a result of local authority changes. Some numbers are bracketed, and in all cases an instruction is given as to which number you should use instead.

In the next chapter we shall go on to look at some simple classification.

—424	Midlands of England

Class here West Midlands; *Welsh Marches (Welsh Borders); *Severn River

For East Midlands, see —425

—424 1	Gloucestershire
—424 12	Tewkesbury Borough
—424 13	Forest of Dean District
—424 14	Gloucester City

Class here Gloucester

—424 16	Cheltenham Borough

Class here Cheltenham

—424 17	Cotswold District

Class here *Cotswold Hills

—424 19	Stroud District
—424 2	Herefordshire

Unitary authority

Including former Hereford City [formerly —42446]. former Leominster District [*formerly* —42444]. former South Herefordshire District. Ross-on-Wye [*both formerly* —42445], western part of former Malvern Hills District, Bromyard, Ledbury [*all formerly* —42447]

For parts of former Leominster District in Malvern Hills District, see —42447

—424 4	Worcestershire

Class here former Hereford and Worcester; *Upper (Warwickshire) Avon River

For Herefordshire see —4242

—424 41	Wyre Forest District

*For a specific part of this jurisdiction, region, or feature, see the part and follow instructions under —4–9

Figure 2.4

3 Simple subjects

Let's start by looking at some simple numbers. For the purposes of this chapter I have chosen some real books whose titles adequately express their subject-matter. In real life, of course, you do not classify something just by looking at its title, and so to some extent this is all slightly artificial, but it is the best we can do in a textbook.

How do you go about finding a number for something that you have to classify? There are two main processes in practical classification:

1 Normally you have to *decide what it is about*, i.e. analyse its subject-matter. You have to do this because you cannot just assume that the title will adequately express the content. You may also need to decide which *aspect*, if any, of the subject is emphasized.
2 Translate your idea of the subject-matter into a Dewey number. Sometimes you will find exactly the number you want in the schedules; more often you will need to follow instructions to construct a number, and this is usually known as *number-building*. Quite often, you will find that you cannot specify all the aspects of the subject that you would like to.

We shall start with some simple subjects which do not require number-building. There are basically two ways of finding numbers:

- Go directly to the schedules themselves; i.e., start by deciding which main class the subject will fall into, then gradually work downwards through the hierarchy until you reach the right number.
- Use the relative index.

You will find that many people take the view that you ought to adopt the first method whenever possible, because this is the only way to be sure that you class the item in the right *discipline* (and remember that Dewey is a discipline-based scheme). However, if you do this all the time, especially when you are a beginner, you will waste quite a lot of time and still not necessarily get to the right place.

It really is a very good idea to use the index; that's what it's there for. Melvil Dewey planned it as an integral part of the scheme right from the start, particularly because this is an aspect-based scheme. It is called a *relative* index because it relates the subjects to the various disciplines to which they may belong. It is a waste if you do not use it. Another important reason for using it is that, however broad a general knowledge you have, you are unlikely to know the place of every subject, and on top of this there are many subjects which in Dewey are hidden in rather unusual places.

➤ What is very important, however, is that you should never classify by using the index alone; you must always find the number in the schedules. This is because:

- when you look at it, you may well feel that it is not the right place after all because the item you are classifying does not seem to belong in that class
- there may be special instructions in the schedules about how to use the number, whether it can be added to, or other conditions.

A good example of the first reason is the subject Acorns. You can find this in the index, but the only reference is to a number for acorns as a coffee substitute at 663.97. Clearly this number would be perfect for classifying something about the use of acorns as a coffee substitute (I have not been able to find such a work!), but for a different aspect of acorns it would be quite wrong. You would have to find another number, perhaps starting with 583.46 Fagales, which includes oaks, but making sure to choose the correct discipline.

Examples

Here is a simple example:

```
Journalism (Geoff Pridmore, 2000)
```

We have to imagine that we can see this book, and that it is clearly a straightforward general book about journalism. If you look up Journalism in the index, you will find that three numbers are provided:

Journalism	070.4
civil rights issues	323.445
sociology	302.23

The second two, however, seem to refer to specific aspects which are inappropriate here. You therefore choose 070.4 and turn to this in the schedules to see whether it is appropriate. It seems to be just what you want.

Another example:

```
Stencilling: a creative home guide (Alison
Jenkins, 2001)
```

Here you find, under the American spelling

Stenciling
    decorative arts   745.73

Again you turn to the schedules and it is exactly what you want.

The relative index

Let's look in more detail at the index; a page of it is reproduced in Figure 3.1 (overleaf). This starts towards the end of a long sequence of noun phrases starting with 'Animal …' and also includes the main entry for 'Animals'.

On this page you can see a variety of different kinds of entry.

    Anis

is a simple entry leading to one number only, 598.74.

Compare this with the entry under Animals. Here we have a long list of numbers, each referring to a different *aspect* of the subject. What do you do if you have a general, all-embracing ('interdisciplinary') book on animals? Well, look at the first entry in the list: it appears *without* a subheading; the number is directly on the first line. This is the number to use: 590.

➤ Whenever you see a subject that has a list of subheadings, look to see if the first entry, the one without subheadings, has a number beside it. If it has, this is always the interdisciplinary number, and the one to use for a general work.

➤ There is still a proviso, however. The work you are trying to classify must contain at least some material that belongs in the class represented by the interdisciplinary number.

Sometimes it happens that there is no interdisciplinary number, and we can see an example of this on the sample page under Animism. Here there are two specific numbers:

Animism
    comparative religion   202.1
    philosophy   147

Figure 3.1

Each of these makes sense individually. It is likely that if anything is written on this subject it will cover one or other of these aspects but not both, and so no interdisciplinary number is provided. If you have to classify a work which covers both aspects, put it at the number for the aspect that seems to receive most coverage. We shall look further at the problems of more than one subject in Chapter 9.

Look at some other entries on the same page.

A few of them refer to the tables rather than the main schedules. You can easily spot these because the numbers are prefixed by the Table number (e.g. T2) and a long dash. The long dash is just meant to show that the number cannot be used on its own, but has to be added to a number from the main schedules.

A simple example refers to a place:

Anjou (France)   T2—441 8

We shall look at the use of the tables in the next chapter.

Sometimes cross-references are shown. This is to help you if you cannot find a number for the aspect of the subject that you are looking for. You may be able to find the right aspect under some broader heading. If you look under

> Animals
> > legendary

you can see that in addition to one number, 398.245 4, there is a cross-reference:

> *see also* Legendary animals

This means that you ought to look at the possibilities provided at the latter heading, as there will be more numbers there. When you turn to Legendary animals in the index you find that there are indeed some more subheadings, and numbers are given which would not be found simply by following the subheadings under Animals.

Terminology

Because Dewey is an American scheme you may sometimes have difficulty with American terminology. And sometimes the index chooses a different word from the one you were expecting, which means that you should always be ready to think of alternative terms for the subject you are trying to find.

Example

> Film (Behind media) (Catherine Chambers, 2001)

This is a general book about film, but when you look up Film in the index you are puzzled by the small number of entries. In this case it looks as though

> Films (Photographic records)   791.43

is the one you want, though you do not usually think of films as photographic records. In this case you might look under Cinema or under Motion pictures, and either of these would confirm that 791.43 is indeed the correct number, as you find when you look at it in the schedules.

► If you cannot find the subject you are looking for, try to think of alternative terms.

► If you still have no luck, think of terms which are broader than your subject, and which might contain it. Dewey does not provide numbers for every conceivable subject, and sometimes the best you can do will be to find a number for a broader subject.

What is included in the relative index

The index is intended to contain the terms printed in the schedules and tables, and it also includes other terms like synonyms, even when they do not appear, provided that there is literary warrant for them. Words that appear only in notes are also included.

Plant and animal names are indexed under their common as well as their scientific names.

Generally, compound terms are entered in direct order, without inversion, so that you find, for example

> Electronic flash photography
> Electronic games
> Electronic music

and so forth, rather than under Photography, Games or Music.

You need to bear this in mind when searching for terms, because there are not necessarily any cross-references. There is no reference from Music to Electronic music, for example.

An exception is that, generally, phrases starting with adjectives of nationality are *not* included unless there is great literary warrant. This means that English literature *is* included, while English paintings is not. This, of course, is because geographical aspects of a subject are usually specified by adding from Table 2, and it is therefore unnecessary to include them in the index.

Proper names

These again have to appear in the schedules or tables if they are to be indexed. The following are included:

- place-names in Table 2
- names of persons who are mentioned in the schedules, which is usually because they define a historical period or have given their name to a philosophical system or similar.

Obviously, if the place-name you want is not shown, you will have to use an atlas or gazetteer to find out where it is, and then use the number for the area that contains it.

Notes

We have already seen examples of different kinds of note in the schedules (p. 12). Sometimes the subject that you are looking for does not actually appear in the heading for the class-number, but is in a note. Sometimes the note says 'Class here', sometimes 'Including'. We will come back to the distinction between these later – it is important – but for the time being you can ignore the difference. Here are some examples:

Examples

```
Angel inspiration: how to change your world with
the angels (Diana Cooper, 2001)
```

If you look up Angels in the index you find that the interdisciplinary number is 202.15. Looking at that number in the schedules you find that it means Good spirits, but there is a note saying 'Class here angels'. You therefore know that this is the correct number to use for Angels.

```
Walking in space: development of space walking
techniques (ed. David Shayler, 2003)
```

Looking in the index you find an entry for Space walks, leading to 629.4584. When you turn to this number you find that it means Extravehicular activities, but it has a note saying 'Including space walks'.

```
Petra Boase's dazzlingly different dough craft
(Petra Boase, 2003)
```

Here there is a preliminary problem in that Dough does not seem to be in the index. However, you realize that it is bread dough, and you find that phrase instead. This leads you to the number 745.5 Handicrafts, where you find the note 'Including work in bread dough'.

Exercises

Here are some simple titles which you should be able to classify without too much difficulty. To make things easier they are arranged in schedule order.

1 The internet (Mac Bride, 1999)
2 Library disaster planning and recovery handbook (ed. Camila Alire, 2000)
3 The Chambers encyclopedia (2001)
4 Philosophy: a very short introduction (Edward Craig, 2002)
5 Tarot: intermediate handbook (Trudy J. Ashplant, 2001)
6 Psychology (Lewis Barker, 2002)
7 Stress management (Jeff Davidson, 2001)
8 Introduction to logic (Harry J. Gensler, 2002)
9 Innocent civilians: the morality of killing in war (Colm McKeogh, 2002)
10 Charismatic glossolalia: an empirical–theological study (Mark J. Cartledge, 2002)
11 Understanding human communication (Ronald B. Adler and George Rodman, 2000)
12 Sociolinguistics: an introduction to language and society (Peter Trudgill, 2000)
13 Economics (Keith Brunskill, 2001)
14 Nuclear power (Ian Graham, 2001)
15 The plague makers: the secret world of biological warfare (Wendy Barnaby, 2000)
16 Modern nuclear chemistry (Walter Loveland and David Morrissey, 2003)
17 Electrical engineering: a concise reference (R. Kories and H. Schmidt-Walyter, 2003)

18 Quiche & soufflé cookbook: a 2 in 1 cookbook that makes these French favorites easy, Rev. ed. (Paul Mayer, 1982)

19 The handbook of human resource management (ed. Brian Towers, 2003)

20 Petfood technology (ed. Jennifer L. Kvamme and Timothy D. Phillips, 2003)

21 Modern petroleum technology, 6th ed. (Institute of Petroleum, 2000)

22 Horse-drawn carriages & sleighs: elegant vehicles from New England and New Brunswick (Richard Wilbur and Peter Dickinson, 2003)

23 Art galleries of the world, New ed. (Helen Langdon, 2002)

24 Beginning origami (Steve and Megumi Biddle, 2001)

25 The counterfeit coin story (Ken Peters, 2002)

26 Painting with acrylics (Wendy Jelbert, 2000)

27 Juggling: from start to star (Dave, Dorothy and Ben Finnigan, 2002)

28 Extreme sports (Lee Linford, 2001)

29 Geography (David Balderstone, 2002)

30 The essential guide to genealogy: the professional way to unlock your ancestral history (Ellen Galford, 2001)

4 Number-building, I: Standard subdivisions

So far we have looked at cases where you find the number you want in the schedules and can use it without more ado. But you will quickly find that such occurrences are actually comparatively rare. More often you need to add something to the number to express another aspect of the subject. This is called number-building, and there are several ways of doing it.

The most widely available is the use of the *standard subdivisions*, which appear in Table 1 in Volume 1 of the scheme.

➤ With an important exception (see below, pp. 36–8), you can use standard subdivisions wherever you like, *without* any special instruction in the schedules. The other methods of number-building depend on specific instructions at the points where they apply.

(The other tables in Volume 1 are used in rather different ways, and *cannot* be used unless there is a specific instruction. We will come to them later.)

The idea of the standard subdivisions is that they cover features that are likely to apply in all kinds of different subject areas; putting them in a table to themselves means that they do not have to be printed over and over again wherever you might want them.

Unfortunately, because of the way the scheme has developed over a long period, they are rather a mixture of different kinds of thing. Some, like —06, —07 or —09, are genuinely subject aspects, but others, like —03, are purely concerned with the form in which the material is presented. Here is a summary list of them:

—01 Philosophy and theory
—02 Miscellany
—03 Dictionaries, encyclopedias, concordances
—04 Special topics
—05 Serial publications
—06 Organizations and management

—07 Education, research, related topics
—08 History and description with respect to kinds of persons
—09 Historical, geographic, persons treatment

Nearly all of these are further divided.

➤ Note that they are all printed with a long dash — in front of them. This is *not* part of the final number, and should be left out when you are building your class-number. It is just there to show that these numbers cannot be used on their own: they have to be attached to a main number.

Let us have a look at what some of them mean, before we see how to add them to the main numbers.

—01 Philosophy and theory

- Useful for theoretical principles, but beware of adding it unnecessarily; it is *not* a way of specifying 'introduction' or 'basic textbook', indeed there is no way of doing this
- Perhaps the commonest of the further subdivisions here are:

—014 Language and communication

because it includes terminology; and

—019 Psychological principles

—02 Miscellany

A subdivision which you would almost never use on its own; it is just a 'hook' for further divisions. Some commonly used ones are:

—022 Illustrations, models, miniatures
—023 The subject as a profession, occupation, hobby
—024 The subject for persons in specific occupations
—025 Directories of persons and organizations
—028 Auxiliary techniques and procedures [etc.]

This again is further divided, and includes

—0285 Data processing   Computer applications

—03 Dictionaries, encyclopedias, concordances

Obvious meaning, for dictionaries of specific subjects; the entries must be in alphabetical order. Do not use for general language dictionaries, which are dealt with in a different way (see pp. 81–3), but *do* use for language dictionaries of specific subjects.

—04 Special topics

This is the odd one out, in that although it is one of the standard subdivisions it has no standard meaning. You can use it *only* when it specifically appears in the schedules, and in each case the meaning is given.

It is simplest to ignore it as far as standard subdivisions are concerned. You cannot predict where it might occur, and you may as well treat it like any other subdivision that is printed in the schedules. The only difference is that it is *among* the other standard subdivisions, rather than being in a separate place.

—05 Serial publications

Another obvious one, and probably seldom used. Most libraries prefer to shelve their serials separately, rather than adding this to the end of the class-number.

—06 Organizations and management

Again, fairly self-evident. It is divided into:

—06   Organizations

which can be divided geographically; and

—068   Management

which is divided into further specific topics related to management.

—07 Education, research, related topics

This covers a wide range of topics, of which the commonest are:

—071 Education
—072 Research
—074 Museums, collections, exhibits

Notice that all of these can be further subdivided.

—08 History and description with respect to kinds of persons

If you are not used to Dewey it can be difficult to understand what this means. It allows you to specify the relationship of the main subject to some particular group of persons, such as young people, or women, giving meanings such as 'women in [subject]', etc.

- —08 would never be added on its own; it only makes sense if you specify *some particular group* of persons, which means that you will always add more digits
- do not confuse it with general history of a subject, which is —09 below
- also do not confuse it with —024 which is used where the work is written with a particular readership in mind
- notice that the note at —082 Women tells you to use this also for feminist views of a subject
- —089 allows you to add from Table 5 for Ethnic and national groups.

—09 Historical, geographic, persons treatment
Undoubtedly the most useful and most commonly used of all the standard subdivisions.

- —09 on its own means 'historical treatment' or 'history of', so that if you have a history of a subject you just add —09 to the number for the subject
- the range —0901–0905 is used for particular historical periods
- for geographic treatment you start by adding —09, and then add area numbers from Table 2 (see pp. 45–7). This is very important because it allows you to specify anywhere in the world, and is probably the commonest use of any of the standard subdivisions.
- —092 is 'persons treatment', which may seem a rather strange term at first sight. It is used to avoid the word 'biography', because persons treatment can be broader than biography. (This is dealt with more fully on pp. 107–12.)

Adding standard subdivisions
How do you go about adding a standard subdivision to an existing number? You just put it on the end; you do *not* do anything to show that it is an addition. Remember that the long dash is there simply to remind you that you cannot use the standard subdivision on its own. The fact that the standard subdivision starts with 0 is enough to show where the subject number ends and the standard subdivision begins.

Examples

> Dictionary of internetworking terms and acronyms
> (Cisco Systems, 2001)

Here we find that there is a number, 004.6, for Interfacing and communications, which is what this book is about. To specify that this is a dictionary we simply add —03 from Table 1 to this, producing 004.603.

> Laughs from the lock-up: moments of humour in
> the lives of prison officers (Evan Thomas, 2000)

The number for prisons is 365, and here we can add one of the lesser-used standard subdidivions, —0207 for humorous treatment, producing 365.0207. Because we have now gone to more than three digits we insert a point after the third digit; this applies in all number-building.

Sometimes after adding something from Table 1 you find that you are allowed to add further from one of the other tables (or indeed elsewhere). Let us look at some examples of this:

Examples

Here is a book which has been written for a particular group of readers:

> The frazzled teacher's wellness plan: a five
> step program for reclaiming time, managing
> stress, and creating a healthy lifestyle
> (J. Allen Queen and Patsy S. Queen, 2004)

This is a book about physical fitness, but it is particularly intended for teachers. The way to specify the kind of readership is to add —024, which then has an instruction to add further from 001–999, i.e. from the whole of the main schedules. In this case we start with 613.7 for Physical fitness, add —024, then add a further 3711 for teachers, producing the number 613.70243711. (The number for Teachers and teaching is 371.1, but of course we cannot have a second decimal point in our final number.)

Use of —024 is perhaps commoner than you might think.

➤ Note that before DDC 22 these numbers using —024 were built in a different way, using Table 7, which has now been abolished. You should therefore be very careful when looking at older catalogue records, as many of the resulting numbers have changed.

That was an example of something directed at a particular *target audience*. You need to distinguish this from works written from a particular *point of view*, or intended to show the relationship between the main subject and a particular group of people. Here is an example of a subject discussed in relation to a particular group of people, in this case women:

```
Feminism and film (ed. E. Ann Kaplan, 2000)
```

This really requires a little knowledge of how Dewey works. In a case like this, you need to understand that this is a feminist view of film, rather than a book specifically about feminism. You therefore look for a number for Film, rather than for Feminism. You find that Film (or Cinema) is 791.43, and to this you can add from Table 1 —082, meaning Women, or feminist viewpoints, producing the final number 791.43082.

Finally we have the very common situation where you need to specify a particular place for your subject. If you look at —091 or —093–099 in Table 1 you will see the instruction to go to Table 2 and add from there for the place.

```
A guide to Chicago's murals (Mary Lackritz Gray,
2001)
```

The number for Murals is 751.73, and we want to specify Chicago. We can add —09 from Table 1, to mean historical and/or geographic treatment, and we then turn to Table 2. Here we find that Chicago is —77311, which means that we can add this to what we have already, making 751.730977311.

➤ You will notice that I have just said 'historical and/or geographic treatment'. When you add —09 on its own, it means 'history of', but as soon as you go further and add the number for a place from Table 2, the notions of historical and geographic treatment coalesce. There is no distinction between the *history* of the subject in a particular place and a general account of the subject in that place. Such a distinction would not usually be helpful.

When there is already a 0 present

Sometimes the number that you are starting with ends in 0 because it is a three-digit number which has a final 0 as a 'filler'. In this case you must be careful *not* to add another 0, even though a standard subdivision would normally have one, *because the 0 is already there*. (Sometimes there is an instruction to use an extra 0; we shall come to this later (pp. 40–1).)

Example

```
The Penguin dictionary of psychology, 3rd ed.
(Arthur S. Reber and Emily S. Reber, 2001)
```

Here you start with 150 Psychology, and you want to add 03, but because you already have a 0 at the end of 150 you do not add another. The result is therefore 150.3.

➤ When you are building numbers and the result has more than three digits, you always put a decimal point (or full stop) after the third digit. This is the only punctuation mark that can ever appear in a Dewey number, and it can only appear once.

➤ Remember to be on the look-out for opportunities to add standard subdivisions, even though the title might not appear to justify one. The work may well not mention in its title that coverage is restricted to a particular place or period, but you need to take this into account and add appropriate standard subdivisions if necessary. This is why it is so important to start by looking carefully at the subject of the work and not relying merely on the title.

Example

```
Social psychology (New directions in Indian
psychology; v. 1) (ed. Ajit K. Dalal and
Girishwar Misra, 2001)
```

Although there is no mention of India in the title, it is part of a series dealing with India, and this would be apparent in examining the book. It would therefore be correct to add —09 from Table 1 to introduce geographic treatment, followed by —54 from Table 2 to specify India, making 302.0954.

When can you *not* add standard subdivisions?

There are some cases where you are not allowed to add standard subdivisions even though you might be tempted to do so by the subject of the work you are classifying. Two simple ones are:

• when a concept which would usually be represented by a standard subdivision has been provided with its own number

- when instructed not to; this is simply a matter of obedience to the printed instructions! (There is of course normally a good reason for it.)

Examples

> Photography: the new complete guide to taking photographs (John Freeman, 2003)

The number for Photography is 770, and when we are used to Dewey we might start by expecting to add standard subdivision —028, which means Auxiliary techniques and procedures [etc.]. If we start by doing this, and check the result in the schedules, we find that at 770.28 there is a note saying

> *For comprehensive works on basic and auxiliary techniques and procedures, see 771*

We therefore turn to 771 instead, and find that it embraces all aspects of techniques relating to photography. This is therefore the number to use in this case.

This is an example of what are sometimes called *displaced* standard subdivisions, because they are displaced from where we should expect them to be and put in a different place. In this case only —028 is displaced.

Here is an example where one of the standard subdivisions is forbidden:

> A hundred years of English philosophy (Nikolay Milkov, 2003)

The number for British or English philosophy is 192. On examination the hundred years in question prove to be the 20th century, and so we may be tempted to add —0904 from Table 1 to represent this. However, there is a footnote telling us

> Do not use notation 09 from Table 1

This means that we cannot use *anything* beginning with —09. The only way in which we might specify the period is therefore forbidden to us, and we have to stop at 192. (The reason behind this is that all numbers in the range 180–199 already imply history, and that therefore to add it again is redundant.)

Note that in this case only —09 is forbidden; we can use the other standard subdivisions if appropriate.

> The dictionary of nineteenth-century British philosophers (ed. Gavin Budge *et al.*, 2002)

Here, although we cannot specify 19th century, there is no problem about adding —03 to represent Dictionaries, producing 192.03.

Provided you read the instructions carefully, and *always check in the schedules every number that you are trying to build*, you should not have any problems about this kind of exception.

'Approximating the whole'

A more important restriction on standard subdivisions occurs when the subject of the item (*before* adding the standard subdivision) is *more specific* than the number that Dewey provides for it. This leads us to the special expression *approximating the whole*, which needs more explanation.

Approximating the whole can be a strange and confusing concept, as is a related term, 'standing room'.

Look at this section in the schedules:

> 025.82 Security against theft and other hazards
>
> > Including disaster preparedness, taking of inventory
>
> 025.84 Preservation
>
> > Including deacidification
>
> > Class here conservation

Example

Suppose you want to classify

```
Disaster planning for rural libraries in
Arizona, Rev. ed. (Michael McColgin, 2002)
```

The number for Disaster planning or disaster preparedness is 025.82. Can you add —09791 to this to specify Arizona? The answer is No, because 'disaster preparedness' does not *approximate the whole* of 025.82; it is only *part* of what could be included at the number, and it appears only in an 'Including' note. It is more specific than the number, and is said to have 'standing room' in that number. In other words, 025.82 is not specific enough for this item. The number then has to stop at 025.82, and you are not allowed to specify Arizona at all.

If, on the other hand, the topic you are looking for appears in a 'Class here' note, rather than an 'Including' note, you *can* add standard subdivisions.

Example

```
Conservation in crisis: proceedings of a seminar
at Loughborough University of Technology, 16-17
July 1986 (British Library, National
Preservation Office, 1987)
```

This concerns conservation in Great Britain, and this time, because conservation is in a 'Class here' note at 025.84, we *are* allowed to add standard subdivisions and so can specify this. The number is therefore 025.840941.

The difference between 'Class here' and 'Including' notes is by no means self-evident and can take some time to get used to. You are advised to consult the glossary in Volume 1 of the DDC to keep reminding yourself about which is which.

The rationale behind it is that a subject mentioned in a 'Class here' note is more or less equivalent to the named subject, and it is unlikely that a separate number will ever be provided for it; usually indeed this would be unhelpful. A subject in an 'Including' note, on the other hand, may get its own number later, when there is more literary warrant for it.

➤ If you have difficulty, remember that 'Including' has Ns in it, and that N stands for No, so that standard subdivisions cannot be added.

No reason for this restriction on the use of standard subdivisions is now given in any of the instructions, but it makes sense if you think in terms of the hierarchy of subject divisions. This gives you a series of steps down, i.e.

> Security against theft and other hazards
>> Disaster preparedness
>>> Great Britain

Because you are not allowed to specify the second step down (because there is no specific number for it), it makes sense not to 'jump' over it and specify Great Britain.

One result of the restriction is that throughout the scheme you will find that compound headings have a note telling you whether or not you are allowed to add standard subdivisions, and whether they apply to the heading as a whole or to individual subjects within it. Look again at Figure 2.3 (p. 16) and you will see this at 684.1044, and at 684.16.

What if you want to add more than one standard subdivision?

Sometimes you may feel that more than one standard subdivision applies to an item. In this case you should look carefully at the list at the beginning of Table 1, and see which one applies first, i.e. which one do you come to first when you read down the list. We shall see this concept again, in the section on Preference (pp. 58–62).

This list has to take account of the differing nature of the standard subdivisions, i.e. the fact that although most relate to subject-matter some are only concerned with the *form* of the material, such as dictionaries. It is clearly more important to add subdivisions which refer to the subject-matter of the work than it is to mention that it is a dictionary, and this explains why —03 appears so low down the preference order.

In other respects the list has been compiled in order to give priority to the aspects most likely to be important.

There is an important proviso here: you must consider the subject analysis of the work that you are trying to classify. A treatise on research into the management of X is quite different from a treatise on the management of research into X, and you *must* take this into account when adding the appropriate standard subdivision. In the first case you would add —068 (Management) first, because research is subordinate to it in your subject analysis, despite the fact that —068 comes below —07 (Research) in the preference order, while in the second case the normal preference order would be observed.

In many cases, you can add only one standard subdivision. Occasionally the instructions allow you to add another, but you should not do so unless instructed.

For example, at —09 you may add from Table 2 to specify place, and after doing so you are then allowed to add from Table 1 a second time, but *only within a restricted list of numbers* given at —093–099 (near the top of p. 214 of Volume 1). This means that if you want to specify a period as well as a place you can add 09 again and then choose a suitable period number from the range given at —0901 to —0905.

What you *cannot* do is add the same kind of thing twice. You cannot specify that a subject is dealt with, for example, in England and France by first adding 0942 and then adding 0944. You can only add for place once; if you add —09 again it must be to represent historical period. For how to deal with this kind of problem see Chapter 9 (pp. 119–21).

Examples

```
New London architecture (Kenneth Powell, 2001)
```

Here we have a book about recent architecture in London. We start with 720, add —09 to specify geographic treatment, and then —421 from Table 2 for Greater London, resulting in 720.9421. But this leaves out the fact that the book is entirely about very recent (1990s and later) architecture. The instruction at —093–099 in Table 1 tells us that after adding from Table 2 we are allowed to add further from the restricted list of numbers just mentioned. It is therefore permissible to add —09049 from Table 1 to specify the period 1990–1999. The final number is therefore 720.942109049.

```
The A-Z of paranormal Scotland [electronic
resource] (Ron Halliday, 2000)
```

This time we find the number for the paranormal, 001.9, and we wish to specify Scotland. We can add —09 from Table 1, to mean historical and/or geographic treatment, and then go to Table 2 to find Scotland, which is —411. This gives us 001.909411. However, we can go further. 'A–Z' implies dictionaries, and because —03 Dictionaries is one of the permitted numbers that can be added after using —09 we can add this, making the final number 001.90941103.

➤ Note that whenever you want to specify both place and period, the *place* must always be specified *before the period*. This is made clear by the order in which they appear in the preference table at the start of Table 2, and it is also a general principle in classification schemes. Sometimes it is not appropriate to add a period number at all.

Many libraries would not wish to add both, because the resultant class-number is relatively long.

Standard subdivisions with special meanings

The other situation in which you are allowed to add what looks like a second standard subdivision is when the first one has developed a special meaning and is used almost like a subject number in its own right. It is then permitted to add the full range of standard subdivisions to it.

Example

Here is a case where the base number, although it looks like a standard subdivision, actually has a special meaning:

```
Mean streets: a journey through the Northern
underworld (Tony Barnes, 2000)
```

This is about organized crime, for which the number is 364.106. Clearly the origin of this is that standard subdivision —06 Organizations was added to 364.1, on the grounds that 'organizations in crime' was another way of saying 'organized crime'. However, it is clear from looking at the schedules that this has now become a number in its own right, and so we are allowed to add standard subdivisions in the normal way. We can therefore add —09 from Table 1 to introduce geographic treatment, followed by —427 from Table 2 for the north of England. This produces 364.10609427.

Extra zeros

I have already told you not to add a zero if there is already one there. However, there are some places where an extra zero *is* required, but whenever this happens you are always given a specific instruction about it. The reason for it, when it occurs, is usually that some extra subjects have had to be squeezed in where there were no spare numbers, and the only way to achieve this has been to use 0 as the first subdivision of a number instead of 1.

Look at this example:

677 Textiles

Here we find the standard subdivisions are in .001–.009 instead of .01–.09, and the reason for this is clear when we look at the place where we should expect them to be. There we find

.02   General topics of textiles

This is a special development of subdivisions which are needed for textiles in general. It could not be put in 677.1 or the numbers following because those numbers were already in use for specific kinds of textiles, and so the only way to get it in here was by using zero. This then forces the standard subdivisions into having double zero, because they always have to come before the more detailed subject divisions.

➤ Look out for this throughout the scheme. The important thing is to make sure that you *always* consult the schedules, because in every case these irregularities will be printed there with instructions.

Example

> Hoo, Howe, Ware, Wye and Wem: weird, wonderful and wacky British place names (Graham R. Irwin, 2002)

'Place names', surprisingly, does not appear in the index, and we have to do some lateral thinking. Under Names we find 'geographic' at 910.014. This is clearly the number for Geography, 910, with —014 from Table 1 to specify terminology added to it (the reason for the double 00 is apparent if you look at the schedules). From this we have to work out that the place names of a specific country will go in the number for the geography of the country, with —014 added. Perhaps there ought to be more instruction about this, but there is not; it is one of the things that you have to get used to.

The number for the British Isles is 914.1, and we wish to add —014 to this. But the schedules tell us to use —001–009 for the standard subdivisions, and the resulting number is therefore 914.10014.

Standard subdivisions printed in the schedules

Sometimes you find that the schedules contain some numbers which include standard subdivisions already printed. There are two possible reasons for this:

- Sometimes the standard subdivision is printed because it is simply a three-digit number, and there is a policy to print all three-digit numbers; see 401–409, for example.
- Otherwise, and more commonly, the standard subdivision is printed because there is something special to notice about it.

The latter may be to tell you:

- to use a standard subdivision in a special way
- not to use it at all, but to do something else (we have seen this already in relation to a 'displaced' standard subdivision), or
- about some special extension of a normal standard subdivision.

Look, for example, at

720 Architecture

Here you will see

    .1   Philosophy and theory

    .2   Miscellany

and other subdivisions printed out.

720.1 is printed because there is a special development, .103–.108, which does not occur at —01 in Table 1 and is a special addition here.

720.2 is printed for a similar reason. In this case some numbers are used with different meanings. For example, —0286 would normally mean Waste technology, but at 720 it is to be used for Remodeling instead. You therefore have to be told what to do with Waste technology.

Further on, 720.9 is printed because in this case you are told that some of the numbers, the ones enclosed in square brackets, are not to be used:

[.901–.905]	Historical periods	
		Do not use; class in 722–724
[.93]	Ancient world	
		Do not use; class in 722

➤ There are two important things to remember whenever you see standard subdivisions printed out:

- The only reason for printing out the standard subdivisions is to *tell you something special about them, or about some of them.*
- The other standard subdivisions which are not printed out *still exist* and are available, so that, for example, 720.3 can be used for a dictionary of architecture.

Standard subdivisions given special modifications

Sometimes one or more of the standard subdivisions may be given some special further subdivision which only applies at a particular place or places in the schedules. You can see this at 792.02. Here several of the normal subdivisions of —022 are given special meanings, *not* the ones that they would have in Table 1. For example, the normal standard subdivision —022 means Illustrations, models, miniatures, but at 792 Stage presentations 792.022 is used for Types of stage presentation, and it is then further divided. A similar thing happens with the other subdivisions of 792.02.

Example

> Create your own stage make-up (Gill Davies, 2001)

This is a straightforward number, using the special development: 792.027.

You will notice that the same division is used at 791.43 Motion pictures, where for the standard subdivisions you are told to use them as modified under 792.01–792.02.

Here is another example. At 796.332 American football the subdivisions —02, —06 and —07 are printed in the schedules, in order to show special developments which apply at this number. Because these developments are also suitable for some other sports we find notes giving similar instructions elsewhere. At 796.334 Soccer (Association football) we see:

> Standard subdivisions
>
> Notation from Table 1 as modified under
> 796.3320202–796.332077, e.g. coaching 796.334077

Example

> Coaching soccer successfully, 2nd ed. (Roy Rees and Cor van der Meer, 2003)

We start with 796.334 as our base number for Soccer. Following the instruction just mentioned allows us to add —077, as used at 796.332, and so create the number 796.334077.

Exercises

All the following involve using Table 1, standard subdivisions, and in many cases you will then need to add something further. Again they are in schedule order.

1 Extraordinary encounters: an encyclopedia of extraterrestrials and otherworldly beings (Jerome Clark, 2000)
2 The internet for physicians, 3rd ed. (Roger P. Smith, 2002)
3 Libraries and librarianship in India (Jashu Patel and Krishan Kumar, 2001)
4 Wise therapy: philosophy for counsellors (Tim LeBon, 2001)
5 Shropshire witchcraft (Charlotte S. Burne, 2002)

6 The HarperCollins concise guide to world religions: the A–Z encyclopedia of all the major religious traditions (Mircea Eliade and Ioan P. Couliano, 2000)

7 Sweet singers of Wales: a story of Welsh hymns and their authors, with original translations (H. Elvet Lewis, 1994)

8 Dictionary of the social sciences (ed. Craig Calhoun, 2002)

9 Encyclopedia of women in the Middle Ages (Jennifer Lawler, 2001)

10 Economics for social workers: the application of economic theory to social policy and the human services (Michael Anthony Lewis and Karl Widerquist, 2001)

11 Secondary breadwinners: Israeli women in the labour force (Vered Kraus, 2002)

12 Career options for law school students (ed. Emily Dunn, 2001)

13 Dictionary of military terms (Richard Bowyer, 1999)

14 Drugs in sport: the pressure to perform (British Medical Association, 2002)

15 International dictionary of adult and continuing education, Rev. ed. (Peter Jarvis in association with A. L. Wilson, 2002)

16 Art nouveau, New ed. (ed. Judith and Martin Miller, 2000)

17 Twentieth-century American art (Erika Doss, 2002)

18 Manchester (Pevsner architectural guides) (Clare Hartwell, 2001)

19 American architecture: an illustrated encyclopedia (Cyril M. Harris, 1998)

20 Aldershot's cinemas (Jim White, 1996)

21 Kenwood: paintings in the Iveagh Bequest (Julius Bryant, 2003)

22 The Penguin dictionary of music, 6th ed. (Arthur Jacobs, 1996)

23 Teaching geography in secondary schools: a reader (ed. Maggie Smith, 2002)

24 International handbook of underwater archaeology (ed. Carol V. Ruppé and Janet F. Barstad, 2001)

5 Number-building, 2: Other methods

We have looked at the use of standard subdivisions in number-building. With the provisos mentioned in Chapter 4, you can use standard subdivisions whenever they are appropriate. But there are other means of building numbers, and these are used only when there are specific instructions.

Other tables

We need to look first at the other tables which are included in Volume 1 of the printed scheme. These are:

Table 2	Geographic areas, historical periods, persons
Table 3	Subdivisions for the arts, for individual literatures, for specific literary forms
Table 4	Subdivisions for individual languages and language families
Table 5	Ethnic and national groups
Table 6	Languages

You cannot use any of these unless a specific instruction is given in the schedules (or in another table).

Tables 3 and 4 are used in Literature and Languages respectively (part of Table 3 is also used in a few other places), and they are discussed on pp. 96–103 and 81–4. Tables 5 and 6 are fairly self-explanatory, and we shall see some examples of their use later in this chapter.

Table 2 Geographical areas, historical periods, persons

Before going further, let's look at Table 2 in more detail, as it is by far the largest and most important of the tables.

We have already seen it being added to —09 from Table 1 to specify place; because this is built in as an instruction in Table 1 you can use it whenever it is appropriate.

The main purpose of Table 2 is to provide numbers for anywhere in the world, or indeed in space, for which you might need a number. Historical periods are also included in brief at the beginning of the table, in order to simplify instructions in some places in the schedules, but you are always referred back to Table 1 for the detail. It is generally simpler to think of Table 2 as dealing with places and persons only.

Most of this is very straightforward, and there is not very much to say about the numbers for the modern world, —4 to —9.

One thing, however, which sometimes causes a problem is the distinction between —41 for the United Kingdom or Great Britain and —42 for England and Wales, because you cannot necessarily tell which the work covers. I should recommend that unless something indicates that coverage is specifically restricted to England or England and Wales you should use —41 rather than —42.

The part of Table 2 which most often puzzles beginners is —1 Areas, regions, places in general. How, you ask, can a place be 'in general'? The answer is fairly obvious when you start to look through the table, and you see that it consists chiefly of two things:

- *kinds* of places, like deserts or socioeconomic regions
- the seas and oceans of the world.

It is unfortunate that the order of the numbers is not very helpful, with all the oceans at —16 coming between the other kinds of area. It is worth remembering —17 Socioeconomic regions, which allows you to specify topics like 'developing countries' or 'rural regions', and this can be useful.

Example

```
Women in politics: voices from the Commonwealth
(Commonwealth Secretariat, 1999)
```

Here we start with 320, to which we add —082 from Table 1 to specify women. (Note that 320 is one of the places where an extra 0 is needed when adding standard subdivisions.) Table 1 at —082 allows us to add further by using standard subdivisions again, and we therefore add —09 from Table 1 followed by —1712 from Table 2, meaning noncontiguous empires. Even then we are not finished, because we can add the area number for the mother country, in this case —41 for Great Britain, producing 320.08209171241.

Moving on in Table 2, the next number is —2 Persons treatment. I will come back to this in more detail in Chapter 8 (see pp. 107–11).

The ancient world is at —3 in Table 2. Notice that not the whole of the ancient world is provided for; the main numbers are for the countries which the western world has traditionally been aware of and studied, such as China, Egypt, the Ancient Near East and the classical world. If you cannot find a number for the country you need, you have to use the appropriate number from the *modern* world, at —4 to —9.

Note particularly that in the numbers for the ancient world —361 British Isles and —362 England, you can *add further* from within Table 2, by taking the digits that follow —41 and —42 and adding them to —361 and —362 respectively in the same way. For example, if the area number for modern Chester is —42714, that for ancient Chester would be —362714. It is easy to overlook this instruction, which is given in the note at —361.

Adding directly from tables

There are many places in the schedules where you are told to add straight from Table 2 *without* using Table 1 first. In some cases you can think of these as more examples of the displaced standard subdivisions mentioned in Chapter 4 (p. 35); it is just that only the geographical subdivision —09 is 'displaced'.

Examples

    Pilgrimage: the English experience from Becket
    to Bunyan (ed. Colin Morris and Peter Roberts,
    2002)

If we look up Pilgrimages in the index we find various numbers. Clearly we want the number for Christian pilgrimages here, so we choose 263.041. Here, however, there is an instruction not to use —093–099 for Specific continents, countries, localities, and we are told to use 263.042 instead.

At 263.042 there is the instruction:

> Class here pilgrimages to holy places in specific continents,
> countries, localities

This work is about pilgrimages within England, and so we add —42 from Table 2 to 263.042, making 263.04242.

    The University of Washington experience (Thomas
    Griffin, 2003)

Higher education has its historical and geographic treatment for the modern world in the range 378.4–378.9, adding from Table 2 directly to 378. We therefore add —797772, which represents Seattle, where the University of Washington is situated, producing the number 378.797772.

> Anglo-French relations before the second World War: appeasement and crisis (Richard Davis, 2001)

This example involves a little more number-building. The number for International relations is 327, and range 327.3–327.9 allows us to specify particular countries. This is similar to the example we have just looked at, in that the notation from Table 2 is added directly to the base number. But if you look at the instruction you will see that you start by adding from Table 2 for the country you want to specify; then, after doing that, you can add 0 and add *again* from Table 2 to specify the second country in the relationship. In this case we therefore add —41 to represent Great Britain, followed by 0 + 44 for France, making 327.41044. This is another case of 0 being used in order to keep other groups of digits apart.

Here is another similar example:

> Russia and the idea of the West: Gorbachev, intellectuals, and the end of the Cold War (Robert D. English, 2000)

This is about contact between cultures, for which the number is 303.482. Here, as in the previous example, there is a special way of dealing with geographic treatment, including a means of specifying the cultures concerned, by adding from Table 2, adding 0, and adding from Table 2 again.

This gives us 303.482 + 47 + 0 + 1821, where the final addition refers to the West. The complete number is therefore 303.4824701821.

Here is another example where a specific 'area in general' is mentioned:

> Mediterranean: a taste of the sun in over 150 recipes (Jacqueline Clark and Joanna Farrow, 2003)

We need to be careful here: the cooking is related not to the Mediterranean *Sea* but to the Mediterranean *region*. 641.591 allows the construction of numbers for Cooking characteristic of areas, regions, places in general by adding to 641.591 whatever follows —1 in —11–19 in Table 2. Luckily Table 2 includes an area number for the Mediterranean region: —1822. We can therefore add 822 to the base number, forming 641.591822.

➤ Sometimes beginners are confused about exactly what is meant by 'the numbers following X'. It literally means the digits that come after X on the same line; it does not mean 'follow' in the sense of appearing *below*, or further on, in the schedules.

In the last example above, it may be easier to think of the final 1 in 641.591 as being the same 1 as the —1 of —11–19, and deal with it like that.

Table 5 Ethnic and national groups

The content of this table is self-explanatory. Remember that you cannot use it *directly* unless there is an instruction to do so, but if necessary you can use —089 from Table 1 and then add from Table 5. (This is comparable to using Table 1 —09 followed by Table 2, but very much less common.)

Examples

```
History of the Arabs: from the earliest times to
the present (Philip K. Hitti, 2002)
```

This is general history, not confined to a specific place or geographic area, and we therefore start with the base number 909.04. Here we are told to add from Table 5, where —927 means Arabs and Maltese, making the complete number 909.04927.

```
Asian American psychology: the science of lives
in context (ed. Gordon C. Nagayama Hall and
Sumie Okazaki, 2002)
```

155.8 Ethnopsychology and national psychology has the subdivision 155.84 Specific ethnic groups. Again we can add to base number 155.84 notation 05–9 from Table 5. We therefore find —95 which means East and Southeast Asian peoples, producing 155.8495.

However, this is a case where we have to read the instructions at the beginning of Table 5 very carefully. Here, the third paragraph tells us that, unless it is redundant, whenever we use Table 5 we should continue by adding a 0 and then add from Table 2 to show where the people in question are located. This means that we can add 0 + 73 to represent the United States, and the final number is 155.8495073.

Table 6 Languages

The uses of this table are naturally rather more restricted, because it applies only when *division* by language is appropriate. (Languages as main subjects are dealt with in a different way: see pp. 81–4.) One major use is in building *base numbers* for individual languages in the range 490–499. Individual languages are themselves divided using Table 4.

Examples

> Early Persian painting: Kalila and Dimna
> manuscripts of the late fourteenth century
> (Bernard O'Kane, 2003)

This book is about *manuscript* painting, i.e. illuminated manuscripts, for which the number is 745.67. We could add —09 + notation from Table 2 if we just wanted to specify the country, but a special number 745.674 allows division by language if required. In this case we add —9155 for Modern Persian (Farsi), producing 745.6749155.

> Francophone studies: discourse and identity (ed.
> Kamal Salhi, 2000)

The general number for Social groups is 305, and this is arranged in order to allow different kinds of division. Language groups are 305.7, and again we add from Table 6 to show the language. In this case we want French-speakers, so we add —41, giving 305.741.

Adding from elsewhere in the schedules

It often happens that the kind of division which you need to make in one subject applies just the same to another. A simple example is Education, where 371.1 contains numbers for various topics, such as Teaching, Academic status, Organization of teaching force, etc. But 372, 373, 374 and 378 cover specific *levels* of education, and naturally many of the same topics crop up again here in relation to these specific levels. You therefore find, at various places in these numbers, instructions to add from numbers at 371.1.

Examples

> Teaching in further education: an outline of
> principles and practice, 6th ed. (L. B. Curzon,
> 2003)

This is about *further* education, which means that we start with 374. Look at 374.11–374.18 and you will see

> School organization and activities in adult education
>
>> Add to base number 374.1 the numbers following 371 in 371.1–371.8, e.g. testing 374.126 ... [etc.]

We therefore take whatever digits follow 371 and add them to 374.1. In this case we want Teaching, which is 371.102; we therefore take 102 and add this to 374.1, making 374.1102.

Here is a more complicated one:

```
Instrumental music for dyslexics: a teaching
handbook, 2nd ed. (Sheila Oglethorpe, 2002)
```

We start with Special education at 371.9 and find that the number for Students with reading disorders is 371.9144, with a 'Class here' note for dyslexia. This number, however, has an asterisk ★ against it, and if we follow this to the footnote we find the instruction

> Add as instructed under 371.9

This refers us back to the instructions given under 371.9 where, among other things, we find

> 3–7 General topics
>
>> Add to base number the numbers following 371.904 in 371.9043–371.9047, e.g. equipment 5, equipment for students with reading disorders 371.91445

So we are now being referred *forward* to 371.904, and we find 371.9044 meaning Programs in specific subjects; this means that we add a 4 (from 371.9044 because we are adding whatever follows 371.904). But still we have not finished because we want to specify Music. We find another note, this time saying

> Add to base number 371.9044 the numbers following 372 in 372.3–372.8, e.g., mathematics 371.90447

So we now turn to 372 and look for the number for Music, which turns out to be 372.87. This gives us 87 to add to what we have already, making 371.9144487.

➤ Always be on the look-out for asterisks and other symbols referring you to instructions in footnotes. Whenever an instruction about this kind of number-building applies repeatedly throughout a range of numbers it is usually given in this way.

As we have just seen, sometimes you have to add more than once, and the number-building can get confusing if you are not careful. I usually find that it is easiest to write down the various numbers (the base number that you are starting from and the others from which you are copying) one directly beneath the other and draw a line so that it is clear exactly what you are adding to what.

$$
\begin{array}{r|ll}
371.9144 & 4 & 87 \\
& \uparrow & \uparrow \\
371.904 & 4 & 87 \\
& & \uparrow \\
372. & & 87
\end{array}
$$

Example

```
Clergy training in Victorian York: the Schola
Archiepiscopi at Bishopthorpe, 1892-1898
(Douglas Emmott, 2002)
```

We start with 230.073 Higher education for specific denominations and sects. We are told to add the numbers following 28 in 281–289. We need to specify the Anglican church, which is 28<u>3</u>, so that makes 230.0733. But because we are adding *whatever* follows 28, and Treatment by continent, country, locality appears at 283.4–283.9, we can go straight on to add notation for York from Table 2, which is —42843. This gives the completed number 230.073342843.

$$
\begin{array}{r|ll}
230.073 & 3 & 42843 \\
& \uparrow & \uparrow \\
28 & 3 & .42843 \\
& & \uparrow \\
(\text{Table 2}) & & \text{—42843}
\end{array}
$$

Adding from the whole scheme

This follows on from the previous section, except that instead of using just a small portion of the scheme you are allowed to add any number from 001–999 to the number you are starting with. A good example is 016, which is used for bibliography of specific subjects. Obviously a bibliography can be of *any* subject, and it is therefore necessary to be able to specify any subject.

Examples

> The bibliography of the Book of common prayer, 1549-1999 (David N. Griffiths, 2002)

Here we start with 016 and then add the number for the Book of common prayer, which is 264.03. The result is 016.26403 because a completed number can never have more than one decimal point.

> T. E. Lawrence: a bibliography, 2nd ed. (Philip M. O'Brien, 2000)

Lawrence is conventionally associated with Arabia in the First World War and is therefore classified at the number for operations in that area, 940.415 with —092 for biography (for more on biography see pp. 107–12). When added to 016 this produces the final number 016.940415092.

Here is a different case where 001–999 can be added:

> Has anybody got a whistle?: a football reporter in Africa (Peter Auf der Heyde, 2002)

This book deals with reporting of football. Reporting of specific subjects is provided for at 070.449 by allowing you to add 001–999. Football is 796.334, so this produces 070.449796334. In this case, because the book is a personal story we can add —092 for persons treatment too, making 070.449796334092.

Note that a number can never *end* with a zero after a decimal point, which means that Bibliography of science is *not* 016.500 but just 016.5 (remember that the zeros are only there to make the number up to three digits; in this case they are not needed because there are more than three digits already, and they make no sense after the decimal point).

Clearly the facility for adding the whole of 001–999 applies only in places where *any* subject from the whole range of knowledge could be relevant.

One of the quite commonly used numbers where 001–999 can be added is 338.47, which is a number for specific services and products when viewed from the economic point of view rather than the technological. You might expect such topics to go in the number for the technology, but in Dewey they do not, and library users can find this very frustrating.

Examples

The apparel industry (Richard M. Jones, 2002)

You might expect this to go in 687, the number for Clothing and accessories, but Dewey makes a distinction between the technical *processes* (which do go in the 600s) and the *industries* viewed from an economic point of view. This book is not about the technology of making clothes, but about the industry, and it therefore calls for 338.47. We add 687 to this, producing 338.47687. In fact the book deals with Britain, and we can therefore also add —0941 from Table 2, producing 338.476870941. Numbers in this section can become rather long, and it may be surprising to library users to find the books in this place. If you go into a large library where Dewey has been correctly applied in this way, you should find a wide range of apparently different subjects at 338.47.

Here is another similar case:

Coping with teacher shortages (Alan Smithers and Pamela Robinson, 2000)

We might naturally expect this to be somewhere in 370 because it deals with teachers, but in Dewey it is the shortages that take priority. There is a number for Labo[u]r market at 331.129, and at 331.1291 we can add 001–999 to specify the particular part of the labour market. (Note that extractive, manufacturing and construction industries are dealt with slightly differently at 331.1292–331.1299.) We therefore start with 331.1291 and add to this the number for Teachers, which is 371.1, making 331.12913711. Then, because this relates to Britain, we complete the number by adding —00941 (note the double 0 required at 371.1), making 331.1291371100941 in all.

Special tables within the schedules

It often happens that a particular range of subjects needs some special subdivisions which are not required anywhere else. Because they are not needed elsewhere there is no point in making them part of the standard subdivisions, but on the other hand it would take too much space to print them out under each subject that needs them. They are therefore put into special tables at certain places in the schedules, with the instruction to add them just to certain numbers.

A typical example of this is reproduced in Figure 5.1:

>   333.335–333.339 Transfer of possession and use of specific kinds of land

> Except for modifications shown under specific entries, add to each subdivision identified by * as follows:
> 2   Value and price
>   Standard subdivisions are added for value and price together, for value alone
>   Class here valuation (appraisal)
> 22   Real estate market
>   Class here economic and social factors affecting exchange of real estate
>   Class price in 23
> 23   Price
> 3   Sale and gift
>   Standard subdivisions are added for sale and gift together, for sale alone
> 5   Renting and leasing
>   Standard subdivisions are added for renting and leasing together, for renting alone
>   Add to 5 the numbers following 333.5 in 333.53–333.56, e.g., share renting 563

Figure 5.1

Examples

> The message of Nehemiah: God's servant in a time of change (Raymond Brown, 1998)

The number for the Book of Nehemiah is 222.8, but we need to add something to say that this is *not* the text of the book itself; it is a book of interpretation. We therefore add 06 from the table given at 221–229, which in turn refers to numbers in 220, i.e. it is the 06 from 220.6. This produces the completed number 222.806.

> No-regret potentials in energy conservation: an analysis of their relevance, size, and determinants (Katrin Ostertag, 2003)

Here we start with the general number for Energy, 333.79. But this is not just about energy, it is about *conserving* energy. There is a ‡ against this number, leading to an instruction to add as instructed under 333.7–333.9. Here we find that 16 means conservation and protection, so we add this to our base number, giving the completed number 333.7916.

Exercises

This time the exercises are divided up according to the kind of number-building that is required. Within each section they are again in class-number order.

Adding from tables

1 Psychotherapy and counseling with Asian American clients: a practical guide (George K. Hong and MaryAnna Domokos-Cheng Ham, 2001)
2 The Knights Templar in Britain (Evelyn Lord, 2002)
3 Methodism in Crewe (O. E. King, 1997)
4 Gods and myths of ancient Egypt (Robert A. Armour, 2001)
5 The identity and role of the German-speaking community in Namibia (ed. Hergen Junge, Gerhard Tötemeyer and Marianne Zappen-Thomson, 1993)
6 Latin proverbs: wisdom from ancient to modern times (Waldo E. Sweet, 2002)
7 Foods of the Maya: a taste of the Yucatan (Nancy and Jeffrey Gerlach, 2002)
8 Arabic typography: a comprehensive sourcebook (Huda Smitshuijzen AbiFares, 2001)
9 Early Celtic art (Paul Jacobsthal, 2003)
10 Journey into the Arctic (Bryan and Cherry Alexander, 2003)

Adding from elsewhere in (or the whole of) the schedules

11 Crystal therapy: an introductory guide to crystals for health and well-being (Stephanie and Tim Harrison, 2002)
12 Ethics and librarianship (Robert Hauptman, 2002)
13 What the book [the Bible] says about sport (Stuart Weir, 2000)
14 Women in science: career processes and outcomes (Yu Xie and Kimberlee A. Shauman, 2003)
15 The European linen industry in historical perspective (ed. Brenda Collins and Philip Ollerenshaw, 2003)
16 Food expenditures by U.S. households: looking ahead to 2020 (Noel Blisard, Jayachandr N. Variyam and John Cromartie, 2003)
17 Choosing students: higher education admissions tools for the 21st century (ed. Wayne J. Camara and Ernest W. Kimmel, 2004)

18 More proficient motorcycling: mastering the ride (David L. Hough, 2003)

19 The horse nutrition bible: the comprehensive guide to the feeding of your horse (Ruth Bishop, 2003)

20 Manual of bovine hoof care (J. Shearer and Sarel van Amstel, 2003)

21 Your outta control ferret: how to turn your frisky ferret into the perfect pet! (Bobbye Land, 2003)

22 100 years of Harley-Davidson advertising (introd. Jack Supple, 2002)

23 Coal – a complex natural resource: an overview of factors affecting coal quality and use in the United States (Stanley P. Schweinfurth, 2003)

24 Ferrous wire (ed. Allan B. Dove, 1990)

25 Handbook of copper, brass & bronze extruded products (ed. Shirley Say, 1977)

26 The golf club: 400 years of the good, the beautiful & the creative (Jeffery B. Ellis, 2003) [About the implement, not the organization]

27 Tennis stamps: the world of tennis in stamps, New ed. (2002)

Adding from tables within the schedules

28 The HarperCollins study Bible. New Revised Standard Version, with the Apocryphal/Deuterocanonical books (ed. Wayne A. Meeks, 1993)

29 Canada's energy future: scenarios for supply and demand to 2025 (National Energy Board, 2003)

30 Reducing underage drinking: a collective responsibility (ed. Richard J. Bonnie and Mary Ellen O'Connell, 2003)

31 A handbook of rice seedborne fungi (T. W. Mew and P. Gonzales, 2002)

32 Sue Cook's bumper cross stitch collection: 12 pictures and hundreds of motifs to celebrate the year (Sue Cook, 2003)

6 Preference order

In Chapter 1 I mentioned the question of citation order, that is, which aspect of a subject is given priority when you are dealing with a compound subject.

In Dewey there are often special instructions as to how to deal with this problem, because

- in many cases you can only specify one of the aspects
- even in places where you can build a number that specifies more than one aspect, you still have to decide which aspect to put first.

In these cases there is usually a list at the start of the relevant section, giving you a list of priorities if more than one aspect applies. Look, for example, at the instructions at the start of Table 1 Standard subdivisions. If you are classifying something where more than one of these would be applicable, you decide which to use by reading down this list and stopping as soon as you come to one of them.

(But remember that, as I said on p. 38, you need to take account of your subject analysis of the work. This may result in a different order of application of the standard subdivisions.)

Another good example is shown at the beginning of 641.5 Cooking (see Figure 6.1, opposite). This is an area where many compound subjects can occur, and it is not possible to specify more than one of them in any given number.

These lists are referred to in Dewey as 'tables of preference' (precedence would be a better word).

Examples

    Quick and easy vegetarian dinners (Grand Avenue
    Books, 2003)

Here we have three aspects:

.5   **Cooking**

Preparation of food with and without use of heat

Unless other instructions are given, observe the following table of preference, e.g., outdoor cooking for children 641.5622 (*not* 641.578):

Cooking for special situations, reasons, ages	641.56
Quantity, institutional, travel, outdoor cooking	641.57
Money-saving and timesaving cooking	641.55
Cooking with specific fuels, appliances, utensils	641.58
Cooking specific meals	641.52–641.54
Cooking by specific types of persons	641.51
Cooking characteristic of specific geographic environments, ethnic cooking	641.59

Class menus and meal planning in 642

For cooking specific materials, see 641.6; for specific cooking processes and techniques, see 641.7; for cooking specific kinds of dishes, preparing beverages, see 641.8

Figure 6.1

- quick and easy ('timesaving' in Dewey's terminology)
- vegetarian
- dinners.

Each of these has its own number in Dewey:

- timesaving: 641.555
- vegetarian: 641.5636
- dinners: 641.54

But there is no way of building a number which represents all three aspects. If you look at the table of preference at the beginning of 641.5 you find that 641.56 comes above the other numbers, and because the number for vegetarian cooking is 641.5636, which is part of 641.56, this is the aspect that is given priority. The number to use is therefore 641.5636. In this case you cannot specify either of the other aspects.

If you think about it you will realize that this placing makes sense, because the book is more likely to be useful with other books about vegetarian cooking than with others on timesaving cooking or on specific meals like dinners. Tables of preference are drawn up with this kind of consideration in mind.

Chemical safety in the workplace: guidance notes
on chemical safety in glass reinforced plastics
fabrication (Hong Kong, Labour Dept.,
Occupational Safety and Health Branch, [2003])

This example is made more complicated by the presence of a specific kind of workplace (glass reinforced plastics fabrication). We will leave that aside, because this section of the scheme does not permit such specificity, and just concentrate on the two main aspects, which have numbers as follows:

- occupational and industrial hazards: 363.11
- toxic chemicals: 363.1791

Looking at the table of preference we find that 363.17 is higher than 363.11, and we therefore choose 363.1791.

Sometimes Dewey does not give a table of preference in this way, but simply gives a general instruction. You can see this at

769.56 Postage stamps and related devices

Unless other instructions are given, class a subject with aspects in two or more subdivisions of 769.56 in the number coming first, e.g. counterfeit stamps depicting plants 769.562 (*not* 769.56434)

In this case we are told to use the number coming *first* in the schedules; elsewhere it may be the number coming *last*. The schedules provide plenty of instances of both systems.

Example

Library services to youth of Hispanic heritage
(ed. Barbara Immroth and Kathleen de la Peña
McCook, 2000)

Libraries for special groups and organizations go in 027.6. The instruction at that number says:

Unless other instructions are given, class a subject with aspects in two or more subdivisions of 027.6 in the number coming last ...
[etc.]

Being of Hispanic heritage would be a minority in the context of this book, which means that there are two possible numbers for this subject:

027.626 Libraries for young people aged twelve to twenty
027.63   Libraries for minorities

Because of the instruction, we use 027.63, because it comes later in the schedules. It is not then possible to specify that this is about youth services.

Not all numbers are like this, forcing you to leave one aspect unspecified. In many places in the schedules you *are* allowed to add further to the base number so as to specify another aspect of the subject. For example, at 577 Ecology there is a general rule to prefer the number coming last in the schedules, but when you choose a number you find that in most cases there are then instructions to add digits from earlier numbers. In these cases, then, a more detailed specification can be obtained.

Another outstanding subject area where complex number-building occurs in this way is 780 Music, which is dealt with separately (see pp. 91–4).

Examples

        Food chains in a desert habitat (Isaac Nadeau,
        2002)

Once again there appear to be two possible numbers:

577.16 Food chains
577.54 Desert ecology

Because of the general instruction at 577, we choose 577.54, but we then see a dagger † leading to the instruction to add as instructed under 577.3–577.6, with the result that we can add 16 from 577.16, producing 577.5416. In this case we succeed in specifying both aspects of the subject.

        Auditing the casino floor: a handbook for
        auditing the casino cage, table games, and slot
        operations (Craig Robinson, 2001)

The number for Accounting is 657, and there is a table of preference for numbers in the range 657.1–657.9. Here the two possibilities seem to be:

657.45 Auditing
657.8   Accounting for enterprises engaged in specific kinds of activities.

The order of preference determines that 657.8 is the number to use, rather than 657.45. Because there is no specific number for casinos, we can go only as far as 657.83 Services and professional activities.

Notice that in this case if the subject had been one of those marked with an asterisk we should have been allowed to add further, and could have specified auditing.

```
Fifth International Dairy Housing Conference:
conference proceedings, January 29-31, 2003 (ed.
Kevin A. Janni, 2003)
```

This is an interesting example. The number for cattle is 636.2. Cattle for specific purposes go in 636.21, with the addition of the numbers following 636.088, so that the number for dairy cattle is 636.2142. But what about the housing aspect: can we specify this? There is no doubt that if we were dealing with cattle in general we could build a number for housing by going to 636.2001–636.208 and adding the numbers following 636.0, giving 636.20831; a similar system applies for most domesticated animals. But the important part of the instruction for our purposes is the final clause:

however, for cattle for specific purposes, see 636.21

This tells us that the dairy aspect has to take priority, and there is then no way of mentioning housing. The final number then is 636.2142.

Exercises

1 Manliness and its discontents: the Black middle class and the transformation of masculinity, 1900–1930 (Martin Summers, 2004)
2 Thumbs up!: inclusion, rights and equality as experienced by youth with disabilities (Catherine Frazee, 2003)
3 Healthcare management dictionary (Annie Phillips, 2003)
4 Recommendations on the transport of dangerous goods: manual of tests and criteria, 4th ed. (United Nations, 2003)
5 Occupational & residential exposure assessment for pesticides (Laire Franklin and John Worgan, 2003)
6 Food chains in a tide pool habitat (Isaac Nadeau, 2002)
7 The food chain (Under the sea series) (Lynn M. Stone, 2002)
8 Small pet health care and breeding (Susan Fox, 2001)
9 The diabetic gourmet cookbook: more than 200 healthy recipes from

homestyle favorites to restaurant classics (Diabetic Gourmet Magazine, 2004)

10 The low-carb barbecue book: over 200 recipes for the grill and picnic table (Dana Carpender, 2004)

11 IT auditing for financial institutions (Jimmy R. Sawyers, 2003)

12 Getting a project done on time [electronic resource]: managing people, time, and results (Paul B. Williams, 1996)

13 Canned cherries (pitted and unpitted) (Elizabeth Rodway in collaboration with the Canned Food Specification Club, 2003)

14 Curve: the female nude now (Meghan Dailey, Jane Harris and Sarah Valdez, 2003)

15 Crocheted lace: techniques, patterns, and projects (Pauline Turner, 2004)

7 Exceptions and options

Because Dewey has developed over a very long period it retains various peculiarities which were introduced before the idea of standard subdivisions had been fully developed. There are therefore many places where exceptions occur to the normal use of standard subdivisions and area tables.

Displaced standard subdivisions

We have already seen (p. 35) the idea of 'displaced' standard subdivisions, meaning that the standard subdivisions, or some of them, are displaced from where you would expect them to be (i.e. the subject number followed by 01–09) to some other position. The usual reason for this, when it happens, is that the concepts represented by the standard subdivisions were given special numbers of their own in the days before standard subdivisions were invented. It would be too much work to rationalize all these, and in many cases it would result in longer numbers, which means that they tend to be left as they are.

Examples

    Libraries in the ancient world (Lionel Casson,
    2001)

This book deals with libraries, not librarianship as a whole, which means that it goes in 027, not 020. We now want to specify the ancient world, and normally we should expect to do this by adding —09 (from Table 1) and then —3 (from Table 2). Here, however, we find an exception, because geographical treatment is specially provided for at 027.01–027.09, where the instruction appears:

    Add to base number 027.0 notation 1–9 from Table 2 … [etc.]

This means that the resulting number is 027.03.

```
20th century architecture: a reader's guide
(Martin Pawley, 2000)
```

This work is general in its geographic coverage, not restricted to a specific country. We would probably expect to start with 720 Architecture, and perhaps add —0904 from Table 1 to specify 20th century. But on looking at 720.9 we find the entry

[.901–.905] Historical periods

Do not use; class in 722–724

We therefore turn to this range, and discover that the 20th century goes in 724.6.

Remember that, because of the general rule that geographic subdivision always occurs before period subdivision, if this book were about twentieth-century architecture in a specific place, the place would have priority.

Another section where historical division is displaced in a similar way is 730 Plastic arts, Sculpture. Here we find that 732–735 are used, in a not very systematic way, for historical treatment of sculpture with a certain amount of geographic division thrown in.

Non-standard areas treatment

In some parts of the scheme you will find that, instead of the normal range of numbers given in Table 2, a variation is used. The result is that —1 (rather than —7) is used to represent North America (apart from Middle America and Mexico, which continue to use —72), so that —11 is Canada and —13 is United States; —2 to —8 are then allocated to the parts of Europe normally represented by —41 to —48, and —9 is used for all the rest of the world (including —972 for Middle America and Mexico, just mentioned).

Again, this situation has been handed down from earlier editions, where these developments took place in isolation from the normal area numbers, because the idea of Table 2 had not been fully thought out. You will notice that the result is to move the United States from —73 to —13, bringing it near the top of the list of countries instead of in its normal position.

Examples

> America's art museums: a traveler's guide to great collections large and small (Suzanne Loebl, 2002)

The number for Art museums or art galleries is 708, where you will see that there is an instruction to class geographic treatment in 708.1–708.9. The United States is represented by the range 708.13–708.19, where the 13–19 corresponds to —73–79 of Table 2 (in Dewey terminology you are adding to 708.1 the numbers following —7 in 73–79). This means that for the United States as a whole the number required is 708.13.

> News and journalism in the UK, 4th ed. (Brian McNair, 2003)

072 is used for Journalism and newspapers in British Isles, or in England, and is therefore the correct number to use here.

> Community diaries: Arkansas newspapering, 1819-2002 (Michael B. Dougan, 2003)

The number for Journalism and newspapers in North America is 071, with the United States using 071.3–071.9, again corresponding to the numbers 73–79 in Table 2. Arkansas in Table 2 is —767, which means that we add just 67 to 071. The final number therefore is 071.67. (There is no particular restriction on then adding —09 and its subdivisions from Table 1 to specify a period division, but in this case the period is so long that it seems inappropriate.)

You must be very careful when classifying in these numbers, because there is a great danger of inserting an extra 9. Read the instructions carefully, and make sure that you know exactly what you are adding to what. For the British Isles the correspondence is particularly confusing, as follows:

—2 represents *either* —41 British Isles/United Kingdom/Great Britain

or —42 England and Wales/England

—21–28 represent —421–428 parts of England

—29 is used for parts of the British Isles other than England, by adding to —29 whatever follows —4 in the relevant parts of —41–42. This makes Scotland —29<u>11</u> (corresponding to —4<u>11</u>), and Wales is —29<u>29</u> (corresponding to —4<u>29</u>).

Remember: the instructions always include an example of a built number to help you.

A problem with these numbers is that because you use up —2–8 for a part of the world which would normally occupy only —41–48 there is then only —9 left for the whole of the rest of the world (apart from North America, of course, which is in —1). Be particularly careful with those parts of Europe which normally occupy —49, because under this system they start with —949. And for anything that deals with Europe as a whole you need to use —94.

The places where this special areas division occurs are:

061–068 (modified)
071–079
191–199 (to some extent)
708
759

At 061–068 there is a further complication because 069 is used for Museology. This means that the correspondence only works as far as 067, and then 068 is used for the rest of the world.

In 191–199 the subdivision is very crude, and does not even allow the addition of full notation from Table 2; you can use only the numbers printed in the schedules.

Prior to DDC 22 there were some other places in the Fine arts where this system applied: 747.2, 748.29, 749.2. These have now been regularized, but you should beware of them when looking at older catalogue records.

More on standard subdivisions

We have already seen (pp. 40–1) that sometimes standard subdivisions are introduced by more than one 0. In most cases this is because some extra subjects have had to be forced in.

Sometimes, however, you will find that there are two 'levels' of standard subdivisions, some with a single 0 and some with 00 (or even more). Again the reason is the same, that a number has been forced to do double duty, and is used for more than one subject.

Example

If you look at 700 you will see that the heading reads

The arts   Fine and decorative arts

The arts are usually taken to include music, the theatre, and sometimes literature too. Fine and decorative arts have a more restricted scope, and are often referred to just as 'art'. A work classed just at 700 could be about either of these topics or combinations. However, as soon as you get to the point of adding standard subdivisions you can make a distinction between The arts as a whole and Fine and decorative arts, because the instructions say that 700.1–700.9 is used for Standard subdivisions of the arts, with 701–709 for Standard subdivisions of Fine and decorative arts.

```
Arts management (Derrick Chong, 2002)
```

This is about the management of the whole of the arts, not simply fine art. We therefore use the double-zero standard subdivision, and need to add —068 for Management from Table 1, giving 700.68.

Irregular use of historical period numbers

We have already seen (p. 38) that it is possible to specify both place and period by using —09 from Table 1 twice; first adding numbers for place from Table 2, and then adding a second —09 followed by the period numbers at —0901–0905 in Table 2.

However, at two places in the scheme, the historic period subdivision is made in a different way. This occurs at 324.9 Historical and geographic treatment of elections and 330.9 Economic situation and conditions, the latter being used for economic history.

In both these places you will see that you start by adding notation from Table 2 for geographic treatment in the normal way. But then, for the period division, instead of repeating —09 from Table 1, you are told (see, for example, top of p. 405 of Volume 2) to go to the main schedules 930–990 and use the period numbers appropriate to the history of the country or area you are dealing with.

This system has the great advantage that the numbers will be tailored to suit the history of the country in question, rather than just being the general ones provided in —0901–0905.

Examples

```
Rebuilding Germany: the creation of the social
market economy, 1945-1957 (James C. Van Hook,
2004)
```

This concerns the economic history of Germany, and therefore goes at 330.943. We specify the period by going to the main schedules at 943 and finding an appropriate number. In this case the closest we can get seems to be .0875, representing the period 1949–1962. The final number is therefore 330.9430875.

```
The economic expansion of the 1990s (Marc
Labonte and Gail E. Makinen, 2002)
```

Though it does not say so in the title, this is about the United States, and we therefore start with 330.973. The instruction on p. 405 tells us that 'in all cases' we should use one 0 before the period number, and this applies even if there isn't actually a 0 in the range of numbers in 930–990 that we are following. The United States does not have a 0 before its period divisions but we insert one nevertheless because of this instruction. The best period number seems to be .929, representing 1993–2001, and so our completed number is 330.9730929.

The easiest way of thinking about this system is just to imagine that the 9 that you already have at the end of the number (330.9, etc.) becomes the 9 at the beginning of the history number, and add whatever you find in 930–999. (In the case of the United States, of course, you need also to insert a 0.)

Note: This procedure used to be much more widespread through the scheme, and there is still the *option* of following it wherever you wish, and not just at these two numbers.

Options

This leads us to consider other options. Generally when you use Dewey you are expected to do what the schedules say, and there is no choice. In many places, however, an alternative is provided.

The options vary considerably in importance and extent, and there is not space to discuss them all here. The ones which I feel are most significant are:

- use of Table 1 —016 for bibliographies of specific subjects instead of main class 016 + number
- use of Table 1 —026 to classify Law of a subject with the subject instead of in 340
- historical period division after geographic division
- options within 340 Law
- literature of specific languages
- biography and 'persons treatment'.

Some places also provide the option of alphabetic sub-arrangement within a number.

In all cases numbers which are optional are printed in parentheses (round brackets). You can see plenty of these if you open the schedules at 789, or at 921 and the following numbers.

We shall look briefly at some of the examples listed.

Use of standard subdivisions —016 and —026
Many people believe that it is more useful to shelve bibliographies with their subjects. I do not agree, because

- it can make them much harder to find, because you are looking for something on the *end* of a number
- if you fail to find a bibliography of your chosen subject it is much less easy to expand your search to find a broader one
- the general rules for standard subdivisions mean that in some cases it is forbidden to add a standard subdivision, which means that bibliography cannot be specified
- in certain other places, such as 759 and the whole of literature, it is forbidden to add any standard subdivision to a number representing an individual person, so that again bibliography cannot be specified.

Much of the same reasoning applies to —026.

Historical period division after geographic division
I have just described this in relation to 324.9 and 330.9, where it is compulsory. It is optional wherever —09 is added from Table 2, and is actually quite desirable, because it means that instead of using the divisions —0901–0905 in Table 1, which have to apply to *all* areas, you can choose numbers that are specific to the country concerned, and therefore more likely to be suitable for its historical treatment.

Other options

It will be most convenient to deal with the remaining options in their several places in the next chapter.

I would strongly recommend you *not* to adopt options, but to use the scheme as instructed. This is certainly the Editors' recommendation, and it also means that you are less likely to encounter problems if you are obtaining catalogue records from external sources.

Finally it is perhaps worth noting that in a sense there is always the option of not following the complete instructions for number-building. You might, for example, decide that you are never going to specify both place and period. Or you might decide never to add standard subdivisions at all. Neither of these possibilities would be recommended by the Editors of Dewey, because there is an ever-present assumption that you will use the provisions of the scheme to the full, but it is not necessarily 'wrong' to make such decisions. If you are using records that show segmentation marks (p. 10) you might decide to break the numbers there.

> What is vital, of course, is that you keep a record of the decisions you make, and stick to them. Any option chosen must be used consistently, and not at the whim of the individual classifier.

Exercises

These exercises do not include use of options.

1 Thinking through French philosophy: the being of the question (Leonard Lawlor, 2003)
2 Britain at the polls, 2001 (ed. Anthony King *et al.*, 2002)
3 The French economy in the twentieth century (Jean-Pierre Dormois, 2003)
4 American economic development since 1945: growth, decline, and rejuvenation (Samuel Rosenberg, 2003)
5 The arts in the West since 1945 (Arthur Marwick, 2002)
6 Becoming an art teacher (Jane K. Bates, 2000)
7 Up close: a guide to Manchester Art Gallery (Michael Howard, 2002)
8 The little book of the Louvre (Brigitte Govignon, 2001)
9 Royal bronze statuary from ancient Egypt: with special attention to the kneeling pose (Marsha Hill, 2004)
10 Continuity and change: twentieth century sculpture in the Ashmolean Museum (Katharine Eustace, 2001)

11 Painting in Boston: 1950–2000 (ed. Rachel Rosenfield Lafo, Nicholas Capasso and Jennifer Uhrhane, 2002)

12 Ireland's painters, 1600–1940 (Anne Crookshank and the Knight of Glin, 2002)

13 Further studies in Islamic painting (Ernst J. Grube, 2003)

14 Australian painting, 1788–2000 (Bernard Smith and Terry Smith, 2001)

15 Dictionary of printmaking terms (Rosemary Simmons, 2002)

8 Special subjects

There are so many anomalies and oddities in Dewey that it would be impossible to cover them all in a basic textbook like this. In this chapter I just want to point out some of the special problems associated with certain subjects, and I will take them in numerical order as they occur.

100 Philosophy

This section is mainly straightforward in use, and contains some of the simplest numbers in the whole of the scheme. There are three main peculiarities to note:

- Historical and geographic treatment is all moved to the end, at 180–199; we have already (p. 67) looked at the irregular notation used there;
- Parapsychology and the occult is included at 130; and
- Psychology is at 150.

Most people would probably not regard either of these last two as being correctly placed, but their position here is historic and is unlikely to be changed.

200 Religion

This class has been shaped by the fact that for most of its life it primarily meant Christianity, with other religions being relegated to 290–299. This is understandable, as most libraries using Dewey, especially in the early days, have been likely to have more works on Christianity than on other religions. In recent editions some attempt has been made to redress the balance, but the bulk of the class still refers to Christian topics.

You need to be careful in looking at the new numbers 201–209. In the first place, these are *not* the standard subdivisions of 200, as they used to be; they have all been reused with new meanings. Secondly, you need to remember that the numbers here refer to religions *in general*; for most of these topics in specific religions there will be other numbers further on.

Within the Christian church, denominations are important, and you will find that in many places you need to specify the denomination before going further.

Example

Mission to West Africa (Patrick Gantly, 2000)

This book turns out to be about Roman Catholic missions, and we therefore need to specify this before indicating the place to which the mission has been directed. The base number for Missions is 266, and to this we add the numbers following 28 in 282–289, giving 2 (from 28_2_) for Roman Catholic. But of course we are not just adding 2, we are adding *whatever* follows 28, which in the case of 282 includes treatment by continent, country, locality. In this case any area notation that we add here signifies the country to which the mission was directed. It would not be clear that this was the meaning of the areas notation were it not for the last sentence in the note at 266.1–266.9. In this case we need —66 from Table 2 for West Africa, making the completed number 266.266.

Notice the distinction between 270 which is History of Christianity, or Church history, and 280 which is History of specific denominations and sects within the Church. This can be quite confusing, and you may feel that it produces some rather unhelpful separations. In practice, when looking at specific countries or regions, it can be hard to distinguish between treatment of a specific denomination and treatment of Christianity as a whole. For example, the Church of England did not come into existence until the Reformation.

Because *any* subdivision of areas notation can be added at 283 and similar numbers, it is possible to go straight into the number for a very specific place, which may seem illogical (especially compared to the treatment of political parties – see pp. 75–6).

Example

The Church of England in industrialising society: the Lancashire Parish of Whalley in the eighteenth century (M. F. Snape, 2003)

Here the area number for Whalley from Table 2 is —427623, and, despite the fact that there is no such organization as 'the Church of Whalley', we can add this directly to 283, making 283.427623.

300 Social sciences
As in 200, the range 301–309 has been redeveloped, and no longer represents the standard subdivisions for the 300s as a whole.

310 Collections of general statistics
This section provides numbers for collections of general statistics, broken down geographically by using Table 2. Remember that statistics of a specific subject do not go here: they go with the subject, with —021 from Table 1 added where possible.

320 Political science
The number which causes most difficulty here is 324 The political process, especially 324.2 Political parties. Here, naturally, numbers are provided for different *kinds* of parties, such as conservative, liberal, leftist, etc. But because it is more useful in a collection to group material primarily by *country*, division is arranged firstly by country and only secondly by the kind of party. This is achieved by adding area notation from Table 2 directly to 324.2, and then adding special numbers (all starting with 0) shown in a table under 324.24–324.29. These numbers for the kinds of parties then become numbers for specific national parties.

In addition to this, certain country numbers are printed explicitly and are given their own sets of subdivisions which override the general ones shown in the table just mentioned.

Examples
        The Conservatives in crisis: the Tories after
        1997 (ed. Mark Garnett and Philip Lynch, 2003)

The number for the Conservative Party in Great Britain is one of those specifically printed in the schedules: 324.24104. We can still add —09 from Table 1 and specify the period, giving the number 324.2410409049.

        Labour in Glasgow, 1896-1936: socialism,
        suffrage, sectarianism (J. J. Smyth, 2000)

This is rather trickier. The Labour Party in Glasgow is not a specific party in its own right, just a branch of the Labour Party of Great Britain as a whole. We therefore start with 324.24107, and do not try to include the number for Glasgow instead of the 41. Again this is a number printed in the schedules. But we can still go on to specify Glasgow at the end of the number by using —09 from Table 1, and we can even repeat —09 to show the period as well. This can theoretically result in the number 324.2410709414409041, though whether any actual library would use such a number is debatable.

Note the difference between this situation, where in effect we are using areas notation twice, in two different positions in the number, and that at 283 which I mentioned above.

We have already seen (p. 68) 324.9 Historical and geographic treatment of elections, which in the geographic section allows the use of period numbers taken from 930–990. The elections may be either local or national, and there is no way of differentiating between these.

Example

```
Local elections in Britain: a statistical
digest, 2nd ed. (ed. Colin Rallings and Michael
Thrasher, 2003)
```

Though not stated in the title, this covers the post-war period, and we can therefore use the period 1945–1999 from 941.085, making 324.941085.

---

330 Economics

Note the difference between 330.09 (History of economics as a subject) and 330.9 (Economic history). The latter is an important number, and the number-building for periods of specific countries has already been mentioned (pp. 68–9).

Notice that 333 Economics of land and energy is part of 330 Economics.

338.47 Services and specific products vs. 338.76 Business enterprises by industry

There can be some confusion between these, especially as there may be genuine overlap. The thing to remember is that 338.76 is used for *specific firms*, whereas more general works about specific industries go in 338.47. In each case it is possible to add the whole of 001–999, but look carefully at the way in which it is done at 338.76, depending on whether the number you wish falls within the range 600–699 or elsewhere.

340 Law

This is an excellent example of the importance of reading the full instructions before 'jumping in' just because you have spotted what you think is the right number in the schedules. In fact, most of the numbers printed in the schedules from 342 to 348 are not correct for immediate use unless you have decided to follow one of the options.

Look at the instructions which are given at the beginning of the range 342–349 (Volume 2, p. 543). These explain that in the range 342–349 a number for a work on law consists of five elements, and that these elements may be put together in a variety of different orders depending on the requirements of the library.

The elements are:

(1) 34, the base number, which is constant throughout Law
(2) a digit indicating the specific branch of law: this is the digit printed directly after 34 in the range 342–349 in the schedules
(3) the facet indicator 0. Although this is rather grandly referred to as a 'facet indicator' you can continue to think of it as just something that is necessary to keep other groups of digits apart, in this case those which appear in (4) and (5)
(4) a group of digits indicating the specific topic within the branch of law referred to at (2); in the printed schedules these appear separated by a 0 from the number for the branch of law
(5) notation from Table 2 to indicate the jurisdiction that the law covers.

The order in which these elements can be put together depends on where the library wishes to place its emphasis.

The Editors' recommended way of doing it is in the following order:

(1) (2) (5) (3) (4)

This is a rather unusual order, however, as it thrusts the geographic division into the middle of the number, in a way which is not common elsewhere.

Because this is rather peculiar there are various other options, as follows:

Option A

This simply omits the area notation for jurisdiction, on the assumption that most of the library's material on law will be on its own jurisdiction and that it is therefore not necessary to specify this. You therefore simply put down the elements (1) (2) (3) (4), which in effect is the numbers as they are printed in the schedules.

Option B

This puts the area number for jurisdiction immediately after the 34, so as to bring all the law of a particular jurisdiction together. It has the disadvantage that if most of the library's material is about the same jurisdiction nearly everything will start with the same number, e.g. 344.2 for England and Wales. This is unhelpful for users, as they need to take more care to distinguish the figures later on in the number.

The order of elements is (1) (5) (3) (2) (4). Notice that the 0 is necessary to indicate that the geographic element of the number has come to an end, because not all countries have the same length number. It is *not* necessary to separate elements (2) and (4) because element (2) can only ever be one digit.

Option C

This puts the geographic division at the end of the number, in the way that is usual throughout the rest of Dewey (except that it is not introduced by —09, just by 0). The order of the elements is therefore (1) (2) (4) (3) (5). Another way of thinking of this is to write out the number as printed in the schedules but *omitting the 0*, then add a 0 and the geographic division.

Examples

```
Immigration: law and practice (David C. Jackson,
1999)
```

The number printed in the schedules for Immigration law is 342.082, but this omits element (5) for the jurisdiction. We shall assume that this book deals with Great Britain or the United Kingdom as a whole, not just England and Wales, and so will use —41, not —42. Numbers for this according to the various options are:

(Standard) 342.41082
(Option A) 342.082

(Option B)   344.10282
(Option C)   342.82041

> Employment law: a guide for human resource
> management (Beryl Grant, 2002)

This too deals with the law in the United Kingdom.

(Standard)   344.4101
(Option A)   344.01
(Option B)   344.1041
(Option C)   344.1041

Notice that in this case the result using Options B and C is the same; this of course is an accident, and should be a warning to you that you cannot just assume that whenever you see 41 it refers to the United Kingdom!

These examples have dealt only with the law of a particular jurisdiction. There are further complications when dealing with international law, but there is no space to cover them here.

---

370 Education

Education naturally includes numbers for specific levels, such as elementary, secondary, further and higher, and there is nothing particularly noteworthy here. A perhaps unexpected thing is that the teaching of specific subjects at elementary level goes in 372.3–372.8, whereas at other levels it is classed with the subject, with the addition of standard subdivision —071. Special education is similarly brought together at 371.9, and particular subjects are included there at 371.9044. The arrangement at 372 bears no relation to the order of 001–999, but this is because it is designed to suit the needs of this level, and includes subjects like Reading. (Optionally you may place the curricula of any subject in 375, but again the recommended method is to put them with the subject.)

Examples

> Teaching children science: discovery activities
> and demonstrations for the elementary and middle
> grades, 2nd ed. (Joseph Abruscato, 2004)

Because this deals with elementary and middle schools it goes in 372. The number for Science and technology is 372.35, and this number has an

asterisk * leading to an instruction to add from the special table given at
372.3–372.8. We therefore add 044 for Teaching, making 372.35044.

> Meaning making in secondary science classrooms
> (Eduardo Mortimer and Philip Scott, 2003)

This, on the other hand, deals with secondary schools, and we therefore
class it with the subject, i.e. 500 Science, adding from Table 1. The addition for Secondary education is —0712, giving 507.12.

380 Commerce, communications, transportation

A particular point to notice here is the difference between 381 Commerce
(Trade) and 382 International commerce (Foreign trade). Each of these has
numbers for trade in specific products, and there is a danger that once you
have created an appropriate number in one of them you may be tempted
to use it for material which should really go in the other.

Examples

> The horse trade of Tudor and Stuart England
> (Peter Edwards, 2002)

This is about a trade within a particular country, and so we start with 381,
not 382. The number for Specific products and services is 381.4, starting
with 381.41 Products of agriculture. This permits division as in 633–638,
which is a range that includes Horses at 636.1. This gives us 381.4161. We
can go further to specify England, noting that standard subdivisions at
636.1 have two zeros. The final number is therefore 381.416100942. (It is
probably best not to try to add further to specify Tudor and Stuart, because
Table 1 —09 does not allow us to be very specific.)

> Banana wars: the anatomy of a trade dispute (ed.
> T. E. Josling and T. G. Taylor, 2003)

This time we start at 382 because the trade is international. Division is similar to that at 381, with .41 again being for Agriculture. The number for
Bananas is 634.772, which gives us 382.414772.

390 Customs, etiquette, folklore

So much has been removed from this section over the years and relocated elsewhere in the scheme that very little remains which is in common use. The main numbers to be aware of are:

391 Costume and personal appearance
398 Folklore

General works on costume normally go in 391, but you should also be aware of 746.92 which is used for Fashion design, and 646.4 which is Clothing and accessories construction. This separation can be quite unhelpful.

398 Folklore includes actual folk literature, which goes here, not in 800. Considerable detail is available in subdivision, showing country and topic. Surprisingly Proverbs, which you might expect to find somewhere in 400, come at 398.9, divided by language using Table 6.

400 Language

The whole of 400 is devoted to Language. General works go in 400–409 and works about Linguistics in 410–419. The latter area in particular is one where the detail in the scheme has lagged severely behind the way in which the subject is studied nowadays, meaning that you find that most rather technical works on specific aspects of grammar just have to go in 415 without further subdivision. This makes practical classification quite easy but does not help retrieval.

Specific languages are all covered in the range 420–490. Dewey gives priority to the languages which an English-speaking library is most likely to deal with, and these have shorter numbers, in the range 420–480. But because there are so many languages in the world the rest of them have had to be fitted into 490 and they therefore have longer numbers.

Numbers for aspects of specific languages are all built in the same way. You start with the *base number* for the language concerned, and then add to it the numbers in Table 4.

The introductory instructions about this are given at 420–490 on p. 896 of Volume 2. Some of the resulting completed numbers are printed in the schedules because they consist of only three digits. In other cases you have to look for an asterisk * against the base number, which leads you to the same instructions. If there is no * you cannot add anything from Table 4. In all cases the base number is printed in the schedules.

The principle is always the same: however long the base number is, you add to it in the same way from Table 4.

Examples

```
Collins English dictionary (2000)
```

This is an 'ordinary' dictionary. We start with 42 as the base number for English. We then add from Table 4 the digit 3 for Dictionaries of the standard language, making 423, and we find that this is printed in the schedules because it consists of only three digits. The number is complete at this point.

```
The Oxford dictionary of word histories (ed.
Glynnis Chantrell, 2002)
```

This is not just an ordinary dictionary; it is an etymological one, which means that we need to specify etymology first. Again we start with the base number for English, 42. Add to this the number for Etymology from Table 4: this is 2, making 422. Then, because this is a dictionary we can also add —03 from Table 1, making 422.03.

```
Basics of biblical Greek grammar, 2nd ed.
(William D. Mounce, 2003)
```

The number for Biblical Greek or New Testament Greek is 487.4. In this case there is no * and no other instruction, which means that we cannot add —5 for Grammar, and the final number remains at 487.4.

Note these particular aspects of Table 4:

- —3 is used for general language dictionaries *not restricted to a specific subject*. For bilingual dictionaries you can add to the —3 further digits to specify the second language. Dewey requires that you classify bilingual dictionaries that go only one way with the language in which the entries are written, which means that an English–French dictionary has to go with English, not French. This is very unhelpful and probably not widely observed in English-speaking libraries. If the dictionary works in both directions you can put it with the language where it will be most useful.
- Language dictionaries of a specific subject go with the subject, and the language aspect is ignored.
- —5 and —82 are both used for Grammar, and this can be confusing. Apart from the subdivisions of —5, most grammar books deal with usage and therefore go in —82.
- —7 is used for nonstandard variations of the language, including dialects and slang, and in most cases you can divide geographically using

Table 2. You must always refer back to instructions at the *base number* to find out what to do.

- —8 and its subdivisions includes numbers for 'readers', books intended to help learners to read. These may be intended either for students whose own language is different, or for those with learning difficulties. In many cases they are specially adapted works of literature, which you might otherwise have expected to be classified in 800 somewhere.

- —9 is normally used for historical or old versions of the language, e.g. 429 for Old English, while in other cases, such as Greek, it is the modern version of the language which goes in 489.

Examples

```
Collins German-English, English-German
dictionary, 4th ed. (ed. Stuart Fortey et al.,
2003)
```

This is a straightforward bilingual dictionary, and because it translates both ways Dewey says we should put it with the language where it will be most useful. For English speakers this will undoubtedly be German. We therefore start with the base number 43 for German, and add —3 to specify dictionaries; we then go to Table 6 and find the number for English, which is —21, making the completed number 433.21.

```
Elsevier's dictionary of amphibians in Latin,
English, German, French and Italian (Murray
Wrobel, 2004)
```

This is a trap. Because it is a dictionary of a specific subject it goes with the subject, though we can add —03 from Table 1 to specify that it is a dictionary. Even if it were in only one or two languages there would be no way of specifying this. The final number is therefore 597.803.

```
Proper Brummie: a dictionary of Birmingham words
and phrases (Carl Chinn and Steve Thorne, 2001)
```

We start with 42 for English, then add —7 from Table 4 for historical and geographic variations. We then have to refer back to 427 to see what to do next. The instruction at 427.1–427.8 tells us to add to 427 the numbers following —42 in Table 2. We therefore find the number for Birmingham in Table 2, which is —42496, and we take the 496 and add it, making 427.496.

There is nothing to stop us now adding —03 from Table 1 to specify that this is a dictionary, making a final class-number of 427.49603.

> Easy French reader: a three-part text for
> beginning students, 2nd ed. (R. de Roussy de
> Sales, 2003)

Here we start with the base number for French, 44. We can add —864 from Table 4 because this is for 'persons whose native language is different from the language of the reader'. In this case the book is for English-speakers, and we therefore follow the instructions given at —8642–8649 and add —21 for English from Table 6, making 448.6421.

In contrast to readers, which you might have expected to be in 800, books about how to write, in particular how to write on specific subjects, go in 808, rather than in 400. (See pp. 95–6.)

500 Natural sciences

Notice the special use of 508. The normal use of standard subdivision —08 is displaced to 500.8, and 508 is used for Natural history. Beware of the way in which areas notation is added at 508.3. (In fact most works on Natural history go in 578 because they are concerned with living things. To use 508 you would need to have substantial coverage of other topics as well, such as geology.)

570–599 Life sciences

The main sections in 500 to look at in detail are the numbers for the Life sciences, 570–599. This section was completely revised in DDC 21, and now provides for the two different approaches to the subject which are adopted today. You should read carefully the relevant part the Manual, especially **579–590 vs. 571–575** (Volume 1, pp. 129–30), which explains the rationale behind the arrangement. There is a fundamental distinction between

- the 'first biology', which deals with the biology of whole organisms, and
- the 'second biology', which looks at the biology of internal processes.

The first biology is the more traditional part of the discipline, which looks at individual plants and animals as a whole; it looks at the general and external aspects of the organisms and is often called 'natural history'. The range 578–599 is used for this, 578 being general and 579–599 for specific kinds of organisms. The second biology deals more with internal biological processes and the structures of specific kinds of organisms, and is often called 'process biology'. The range 571–575 is used for this.

(Between the two groups come 576 Genetics and evolution and 577 Ecology.)

When you look at the ways in which numbers are built within each of the two ranges mentioned, it can at first view appear confusing, and you can start to wonder whether it is possible to build numbers for compound subjects in both directions at once. When you work it out carefully you will find that this cannot happen.

If you look at 571.1 Physiology of animals and 571.2 Physiology of plants and microorganisms, you will see that in each case you can add digits from numbers further on in the scheme in order to specify particular animals or plants when required. A similar arrangement then applies at other numbers marked with an asterisk * in the range 572–575. Conversely, in those numbers in the range 579–599 that cover all the individual plants and animals, you can add digits from earlier numbers *in the same range*, but not from 571–575.

This means that in each case the subjects are different and there is no overlap. The result of this is that, depending on what compound subject you are trying to specify, you will build the number sometimes starting from the process in 571–575 and sometimes starting from the specific plant or animal in 579–599. Some examples should make this clearer.

Examples

> Physiological systems in insects (Marc J.
> Klowden, 2002)

Physiology is 571, and Physiology of animals 571.1. Here we can add the numbers following 59 in 590.1–599, which allows us to specify Insects. The number for Insects is 59<u>5.7</u>, and so we add the 57, making 571.157.

Suppose we tried to start with Insects at 595.7. We can add as instructed under 592–599, but the instructions there do not allow any addition from 571, only from a limited range in 591. There is therefore no way of building the correct number from that starting-point.

> Responses of plants to UV-B radiation (ed. Jelte
> Rozema, Yiannis Manetas and Lars-Olof Björn,
> 2001)

The number for effects of ultraviolet radiation on organisms is 571.456, and this has an asterisk * and the usual instruction to add as instructed at 571–572. This means that in this case we add 2 for plants, giving the completed number 571.4562.

Again, let's look at what would happen if we tried to start somewhere else. The general number for Plants is 580, but special topics go in 581, which allows number-building. It does not, however, provide any way of specifying the biophysical aspects that are covered at 571.4, and this shows that it is the wrong starting-point.

```
Fish adaptations (ed. Adalberto Luis Val and B.
G. Kapoor, 2003)
```

Here is an example where we need to start from the number for the creature concerned, in this case 597 Fishes. The note tells us to add as instructed at 592–599, which means that we can add 1 for 'General topics of natural history of animals', making 597.1, and then add whatever follows 1 in 591.3–591.7. The number there for Adaptation is 591.4, which gives us the final number 597.14. Again, if we tried to start this from 591.4 we would find that there is then no way of specifying fish.

As a relief, you may like an example where no number-building is necessary at all.

```
Biomimicry [videorecording]: learning from
nature (Bullfrog Films, 2002)
```

Because this is not restricted to any particular animal, it just goes in 591.473.

---

600 vs. 700

Numbers in 600 cover a very wide range of subjects, and in many cases they cover both processes and products. For example, 629.222 Passenger automobiles would be used both for works about building cars and for works about cars themselves. There can be a tendency to forget this because some subjects crop up again in 700 when viewed as products of the fine arts. 666.3 Pottery and 738 Ceramic arts are a particularly unsatisfactory pair as far as the hand-production period is concerned; one really does not want two different numbers for this subject. When such a pair exists, it is better to use the number in 600 for the more technical, or manufacturing, aspects.

See in particular the note on 745.5928 in the Manual (Volume 1, p. 150).

610 Medicine and health

You need to remember that social welfare aspects of medical problems go in 362.1. Materials about human physiology, the diseases themselves and the methods of treating them go in the various divisions of 610. This means that the usual number for Drug abuse is 362.29, whereas the coverage of drugs that a pharmacist or medical practitioner would need goes in 615.

Notice that 610.73 Nursing, though originally a standard subdivision of 610, is a number in its own right and not only can have standard subdivisions added to it but also has many other specific divisions.

The most substantial part of this section is 616.1–616.9 Specific diseases. Here you will see a special table which provides numbers that can be added to any number marked with an asterisk * in the schedules. These include 05 Preventive measures and 06 Therapy, in each of which considerable number-building takes place.

These topics come up again in relation to 618.92 Pediatrics and 618.97 Geriatrics, both of which provide for number-building using the elements from 616.

Examples

```
Hip replacement [electronic resource]: current
trends and controversies (ed. Raj K. Sinha,
2002)
```

The number for Hips is 617.581, and this is marked with an asterisk * meaning that we can add as instructed under 617. Here the most appropriate addition is 0592 which is used for Cosmetic and restorative plastic surgery, etc., including 'implantation of artificial organs'. The final number is therefore 617.5810592.

```
Hip disorders in childhood (ed. John V. Banta
and David Scrutton, 2003)
```

Because this concerns children we start with 618.92 Pediatrics. Here the number for Regional medicine (which means relating to parts of the body) is 618.920975, to which we add the numbers following 617.5. We have already seen that the number for Hips is 617.5<u>81</u>, which this time gives us 618.92097<u>581</u>.

---

630 Agriculture and related technologies

We have looked at 570–599 for the Life sciences; that section deals with plants and animals as they occur naturally. 630 on the other hand deals with plants and animals as far as they are used by humans. There is no distinction between the different uses of animals (as pets or kept for food, fur, etc.), though to some extent this can be specified by number-building. We have already seen some examples of number-building and preference in this section (p. 62).

700 The arts   Fine and decorative arts

Several of the noteworthy features of this class have already been mentioned:

- 700 on its own has to mean both The arts as a whole and Fine and decorative arts, but the two ranges of standard subdivisions 700.1–700.9 and 701–709 make the distinction (see pp. 67–8)
- non-standard areas notation at 708 and 759 (see pp. 65–7)
- non-standard period notation (partly combined with geographic division) in 720 (722–724) and 730 (732–735) (see p. 65)
- modifications to some standard subdivisions at 791.43 and 792 (see pp. 42–3).

Later we shall see that persons treatment varies markedly in different parts of the class (pp. 109–10). Other points to note are:

700.4 Special topics in the arts

This is one of the areas outside Literature where Table 3C is used. Be careful to differentiate 700.4 from 704, which deals purely with the fine and decorative arts.

Example

```
Flight: a celebration of 100 years in art and
literature (ed. Anne Collins Goodyear, 2003)
```

Because this includes both art and literature this combination counts as The arts as a whole, which means that we use 700.4. We go to 700.42–700.48 Arts dealing with specific themes and subjects, and add from Table 3C the numbers following —3. There we find –356 Technical themes, with a note 'Including flight, ships', and so we add 56, making the final number 700.456.

---

704 Special topics in fine and decorative arts

Because 708 has been used for Galleries, the normal standard subdivision —08 for Fine and decorative arts is displaced to 704.03–704.08.

But the main part of 704 is 704.9 Iconography. One frequent requirement in classifying in the Fine arts is that of specifying pictures of particular subjects, and that is what this number means.

Be careful, however: if the item you are classifying is restricted to some particular form within the fine arts, such as drawings, paintings, engravings or photographs, then you must class it in the appropriate number for the form, divided by subject if such provision is available.

Examples

```
Animals in art (Bridget Crowley, 2003)
```

This is a simple one, because the number is printed in the schedules: 704.9432.

This is more interesting:

```
Dinosaur imagery: the science of lost worlds and
Jurassic art: the Lanzendorf collection
(foreword by Philip J. Currie; photography by
Michael Tropea, 2000)
```

Again we start with 704.9432 which is Animals in art. Can we specify dinosaurs? Looking at 704.94322–704.94329 we see that it is possible to specify particular animals by adding the numbers following 59 in 592–599. However, the number for dinosaurs is 567.9, which does not fall within that range. This means that we have to stop at 704.9432 after all.

You might object that 704.949 allows us to add the whole of 001–999 in order to specify *any* subject, and we could therefore create 704.9495679. I take the view that because Animals are specified as a subject, and dinosaurs were animals, they should go there; it is not helpful to separate them from the rest of animals.

---

709 Historical, geographic ... treatment of fine and decorative arts

Works on European art of specific periods go in 709.01–709.05, rather than in 709.4. This is highly irregular, and means that a geographic division is being implied when only the period numbers are expressed. It doubtless owes its origin to the fact that most Western art history has been predominantly Europe-centred. Only comprehensive works on European art not restricted to a particular period go in 709.4; this is unsatisfactory, because not only are they separated from the others, it means that a more general topic comes *after* a more specific.

720 Architecture

Note the special table at 721 which permits further subdivision of numbers in the range 725–728. The 'Class here' note for architectural drawings for —0222 is also useful; notice that you can then add from Table 2 to show where the drawings are from.

750 Painting and paintings

You will see that 751 is Techniques, procedures, apparatus, equipment, materials, forms, which is rather a mixture. The numbers at 751.4 are used for the techniques *only*, and not for the final results. A book consisting of watercolours would not go here. It would go in 750 or the range 753–759 according to its subject-matter and according to the table of preference at the beginning of 750.

At 751.7 Specific forms, however, the numbers *are* used for the final results, which means that a book of murals, or about murals, would go here, provided that it did not fall within the range 753–758, which is higher in the preference order.

Examples

> The watercolour waterscape painter's pocket palette: practical visual advice on how to create waterscapes using watercolours (Joe Francis Dowden, 2003)

This is about *how to paint* waterscapes in watercolour, not a book of pictures of them. It therefore goes in 751.422 Watercolo[u]r painting. However, 751.4224 allows you to specify subjects, which you do by adding from 704.94 Iconography of specific subjects. The number for marine scenes and seascapes there is 704.94<u>37</u>, which means that you add 37, producing 751.422437.

By contrast

> Marine painting: images of sail, sea and shore (James Taylor, 2002)

is a book of marine paintings, rather than a 'how to' book. It therefore goes in 758.2.

There is obviously some overlap between the two types, but you should be careful to avoid classifying works on techniques in 753–758.

770 Photography, photographs, computer art

We have already noticed the displacement of part of standard subdivision —028 to 771; 772–775 are also used for specific processes. 776 has been introduced in DDC 22 for Computer art, which is not an ideal placing as it intrudes in the middle of Photography.

Persons treatment in 770 is mentioned later (see p. 110).

The main distinction to be aware of is between 778.9 and 779. The first is restricted to techniques, i.e. how to take photographs of a specific subject, whereas collections of actual photographs go in 779. In each case the system of division is the same, using the numbers following 704.94 in 704.942–704.949.

Examples

    `Creative canine photography (Larry Allan, 2003)`

This is about taking photographs of dogs, and so we start with 778.9. We then add the numbers following 704.94 in 704.942–704.949. Animals are 704.9432, but we can go further and specify dogs, by adding the numbers following 59 in 592–599. Dogs are 599.<u>772</u>, which gives us 704.9432<u>9772</u>. Transferring this to 778.9 we arrive at 778.9329772.

    `People in Vogue: a century of portraits (ed.`
    `Robin Derrick and Robin Muir, 2003)`

This is simply a collection of portraits from the magazine *Vogue*. We need do no more than specify portraits, which means that 704.94<u>2</u> leads to 779.<u>2</u>.

---

780 Music

Music is one of the most complex parts of the scheme, having been redeveloped in DDC 20 in order to allow extensive number-building, and it is impossible here to go into all the details. It is rather like the Life sciences in that the numbers can be grouped into different ranges. These are:

780–781	General principles and musical forms
782–783	Vocal music
784–788	Instrumental music
789	reserved for optional use for Composers and traditions of music

This sequence is designed so that numbers for the recurrent topics which apply to all kinds of music are included in 781; elements from these numbers can then be attached to the numbers for specific voices and instruments in the ranges further on. Look carefully at the instructions given at 780 in the schedules, and at the further information in the Manual.

You will notice three main points:

- Unless other instructions are given, you should class a subject with aspects in two or more subdivisions of 780 in the number coming *last*; this will always be the starting-point for your number-building, and you will usually be able to add digits from numbers appearing *earlier* in the schedule.
- Both 0 and 1 are used as 'facet indicators', i.e. ways in which the separate elements in the number-building are kept distinct; this again is like 570–590.
- In building a number, you should not add 0 or 1 more than twice altogether; this will sometimes mean that another aspect remains unspecified, but it is intended to prevent unduly long numbers. (Optionally you may add as often as you wish.)

You should look carefully through the examples of number-building in the Manual (pp. 152–4), because these are very helpful.

A particular problem with Music, which does not affect most other subjects, is that there is usually a practical distinction between music itself and works *about* music. Dewey does not take account of this because it is assumed that the physical format of the material usually necessitates a separation of sequences in a collection. Most libraries with music collections would usually have at least the following sequences:

- books about music
- musical scores (sheet music)
- miniature scores (reduced-size versions of scores, intended primarily for study)

- sound recordings (probably divided into separate sequences according to physical format).

These sequences would probably be differentiated by means of prefixes to the Dewey numbers. (Optionally, you can use a set of subdivisions of —026 which are listed under 780.26, but the normal purpose of these is for *texts* about those formats, not for the formats themselves. In any case, doing this assumes that all the sequences are interfiled, which is unlikely. Look at the entry for **780.26** in the Manual (p. 155) for an explanation of these.)

The way the general arrangement works means that because priority is given to the voice or instrument it is impossible to make a primary distinction between 'classical' and 'popular' music. These will therefore be found repeatedly throughout the range, which many libraries may find unhelpful.

Number-building in 780

The key principle is that you always start with the number that appears *latest* in the schedules, and work backwards.

Examples

        The art of piano pedaling: two classic guides
        (Anton Rubinstein and Teresa Carreño, 2003)

The number for Piano is 786.2, and we see that it is marked with an asterisk ★ leading to the instruction to add as instructed under 784–788. This takes us to the instruction to add 18–19 from 784 for Musical forms and instruments. Luckily there is a note in the instruction at 11–17 referring us to 193 for techniques for playing instruments, otherwise we might not think that 18–19 was the right place to look at all. Turning to 784.1 we find 784.1938 means Leg techniques, 'Including pedaling', and we can therefore complete the number as 786.21938.

Here is a more straightforward one:

        The BBC Proms pocket guide to great symphonies
        (ed. Nicholas Kenyon, 2003)

The number for Symphonies is 784.184, and this is satisfactory for this general treatment of the subject.

        The Virgin encyclopedia of popular music,
        Concise 4th ed. (ed. Colin Larkin, 2002)

Because this is about *all* kinds of popular music, it is easy to classify: in the general number for Popular music at 781.63. We can add —03 from Table 1 because it is an encyclopedia, making 781.6303.

> Bing Crosby: crooner of the century (Richard Grudens, 2003)

This is about a singer, and so we start with 782.42. But he was a singer specifically of popular music, and we need to specify this. Following the instructions, we add as instructed at 782.1–782.4, and are again led back to 781.64 Western popular music. This produces 782.42164, where again we add as intructed: this time —092 for Persons treatment, making 782.42164092. Different kinds of singer would get different numbers, but all starting from 782.42.

Be very careful when following the 'Add' instructions. When you add 1 for General principles and musical forms, in the range 11–17 you are following 781.1–781.7, but in 18 it is *784*.18. Similar distinctions apply throughout 780 when following similar instructions, and you must make sure that you are looking at the correct range of numbers.

Another point to notice is that the numbers in the range referring to instruments, 786–788, refer to *music* for those instruments, not to the instruments themselves. If you have something about the instrument itself, its history, construction and other matters, you need to add 19 and its subdivisions from 784.19, and there will always be an instruction if you are allowed to do this.

Example

> A history of the organs in St Paul's cathedral (Nicholas Plumley and Austin Niland, 2001)

The number for Organs is 786.5, and this has the usual 'Add' instruction. Musical forms and instruments involves adding from 784.18–784.19, where .19 is Instruments. Geographic treatment then goes in .194–.199, which means that you use 194212 for the City of London, making 786.5194212. You might have been tempted to go for 786.5094212, but this would mean (if it means anything) organ music in the City of London, rather than organs.

791.43 Motion pictures

791.43 is another place where Table 3C can be used to specify films displaying specific qualities, themes and subjects.

Example

> ```
> British horror cinema (ed. Steve Chibnall and
> Julian Petley, 2002)
> ```

The number for Special aspects of films is 791.436, and Films displaying specific qualities is 791.4361, to which we add the numbers following —1 in 11–17 in Table 3C. This gives —1<u>64</u> for Horror, which means that we add 64; we can then also add —0941 to specify British, making the completed number 791.4361640941.

---

800 Literature

The range 800–809 is used for Literature in general, or for collections or criticism relating to more than two individual literatures. The rest of the 800s, 810–890, is devoted to individual literatures, that is, to literatures related to specific languages. To a great extent there is a correspondence between these numbers and those in 420–490 for the languages themselves. For example, 450 means Italian language, and 850 Italian literature.

Let us look first at 800–809. The chief thing to note here is the use of numbers starting in 808.0 for some topics which you might not think of as literature at all, especially works about *how to write*. 808.066 covers how to write about specific subjects, and allows you to add 001–999 from the whole scheme to specify the subject, *but only up to three digits*. This restriction is because you are then allowed to add 0 and notation from Table 6 to specify the language concerned.

Examples

> ```
> Writing and presenting scientific papers
> (Birgitta Malfors et al., 2000)
> ```

We start with 808.066 and add 5 (from 500) to specify Science. We could in theory add 0 and —21 from Table 6 to specify English, but I suspect that most libraries would use this provision only in relation to foreign languages. I therefore suggest that we stop at 808.0665.

Here is a more complex example:

```
Exito comercial: prácticas administrativas y
contextos culturales (Michael Scott et al.,
2001)
```

Again we start with 808.066 and add 651 for Office services to this. Because the work is about writing in Spanish we then add 0 and turn to Table 6 for the number for Spanish, —61, making 808.066651061.

Also at 808.8–809 we have the numbers for collections of literature and criticism where the literatures of more than two languages are concerned. Numbers can be built to specify the subject, period, intended audience and other aspects. The way in which this is done is in many ways similar to the method used for individual literatures (see below, pp. 100–3), but there is not space in this book to go into it in detail.

810–890 Literatures of specific languages and language families

Let us now move on to the individual literatures in 810–890. Here classifying can be very simple, or extremely complex. To some extent this depends on the answer to the following question, which is the first thing you need to ask yourself about anything that you are trying to classify in this area:

- Is it a work or works by or about an *individual* writer? or
- Is more than one writer involved?

This distinction will determine how you go about building the number.

In the first case you will make use of Table 3A, and in the second Table 3B, with possible addition from Table 3C.

Works by or about an individual writer

Notice that it is *by or about*. The intention is that criticism of individual works by an author, or of the author's works as a whole, should be shelved with the works themselves. Most libraries will separate authors from each other by arranging them alphabetically within their class-number, but this is not specifically dealt with in Dewey.

A very important point to note is that *for works by or about an individual author* you cannot specify the *subject-matter*. This means that you do not have to determine what a book of poems is about, or decide whether a novel is a romance or a detective story. Nor do you have to take account of the fact that a biography or critical work might focus on a particular aspect of the writer's life. All this is irrelevant for individual authors. (For collections and criticism the situation is different; see below, pp. 100–3.)

To build a number for an individual author you need three elements:

- the base number for the literature in question (based on which *language* it is in)
- a single digit indicating the *literary form* of the work (poems, fiction, etc.)
- a number indicating the *period* in which the work was written.

This is a very straightforward procedure. Note that it separates an author's works according to their literary form, so that if an author writes both poetry and plays these will have different numbers, and will not be together on the shelves. Many academic libraries feel that it would be more useful to give more priority to period, rather than literary form, but this is not the way Dewey works.

Base number

You need to decide which literature is involved. This is not usually a problem, but note that American and British literature in English are regarded as separate, using 810 and 820 respectively.

Translations are, or should be, treated as if they were in the *original* language.

Using the numbers in the range 810–890 you have to find the *base number* for your literature. As we saw with languages, *not all base numbers have the same number of digits*; this is inevitable in view of the number of literatures which exist. The base number for English is 82, whereas for Russian it is 891.7, and for Swahili it is 896.392. *This makes no difference to the way in which you build the number.*

Remember that the final 0 in the numbers at 820, etc. is only there as a filler to make the number up to three digits; the base number itself is 82, and it is to this that you add the next part.

Number for literary form

For most languages you take these from Table 3A. They are as follows:

1 Poetry
2 Drama
3 Fiction
4 Essays

5 Speeches
6 Letters
8 Miscellany

(870 Classical Latin and 880 Classical Greek work in a slightly different way. Look at the schedules.)

You will find that 1, 2 and 3 are the most commonly used numbers. Notice the table of preference which ensures that plays written in verse are treated as drama, not poetry. 5 and 6 seldom occur nowadays. 6 is used only for letters written *as literature*, not for actual correspondence. You will see that 7 does not exist for individual writers.

You choose whichever of these is appropriate and add it to the base number that you already have, e.g.

82 + 3 = 823 English fiction
891.7 + 3 = 891.73 Russian fiction
896.392 + 3 = 896.3923 Swahili fiction

Period number

Here you have to turn back to the main schedules, from which you took the base number in the first place. You will find that each literature has its own set of period numbers, which are specially designed to suit the history of that literature. You need to choose the one that most closely matches the period of your author's works. It is essential that all of an author's works have the same period number; you do not change numbers according to the actual dates of individual works. The normal procedure is to choose the period number appropriate to the person's first major work, though there are occasional exceptions to this.

Some minor literatures have no period numbers because there is not enough material to justify further division. In these cases you stop when you have added the number for literary form.

(Optional treatment: If, for example, you want to separate the various literatures that use English, the option on pp. 778–9 of Volume 3 allows you to do this by prefixing the class-number with a letter, and then using different period numbers for each language.)

When you have added the period number, your number is complete, *unless* the number for literary form which you added was 8. In this case – which is quite rare – you need to add further *after* the period number. The additions are shown in Table 3A; you will notice that they all start with 0 because they have to be kept distinct from the period numbers. Because there is otherwise no general number for Prose, that appears here, at 8∪08. (I am using the symbol ∪ here to show that the numbers form part of a single unit, which happen to be separated by having the period number within them; this is not part of the Dewey notation.) Perhaps the most useful of these numbers is 8∪09 which is used for works *about* an individual writer who is not known primarily for any specific literary form. This is unique in that it is used only for works *about*, not for works *by*, the author.

Examples

```
The collected poems of John Donne (ed. Roy
Booth, 2002)
```

Donne was an English poet, so we start with 82, add 1 for Poems, and complete the number with 3 for the Elizabethan period 1558–1625. This produces the complete number 821.3.

```
City: an essay (Brian Lennon, 2002)
```

This is an essay by an American writer, and so we start with 81. Add 4 for Essays, then the period number 6 for 2000–, producing 814.6.

```
Chaucer's church: a dictionary of religious
terms in Chaucer (Edward E. Foster and David H.
Carey, 2002)
```

On first view you might perhaps expect this to go in Religion somewhere, but because the focus of the book is Chaucer, and Chaucer is primarily remembered as a poet, that is where it goes. Start again with 82, add 1 for poetry, then 1 for the period 1066–1400, making 821.1. In this case we cannot specify the fact that it is about religious terms, or that it is a dictionary, because all works by or about an individual writer have to go at the same number.

```
The prose works of Andrew Marvell (ed. Martin
Dzelzainis and Annabel Patterson, 2003)
```

Because this is prose it calls for the use of 8∪08. The base number for English is again 82, to which we add the first 8. We then have to put the appropriate period number for Marvell, which is 4 (1625–1702) and then the remaining 08, to produce 828.408.

Shakespeare

Because he is so famous, Shakespeare actually has his own number in English drama, namely 822.33. This does not apply in Poetry, which means that a book of his sonnets goes in 821.3, because 821.33 does not exist.

(There is also the *option* of using 822.33 for all his works, including poetry, and using an alphabetical arrangement to give some structure to the sequence of works. See Volume 3, pp. 779–80.)

Collections or criticism of more than one writer

Some of the numbers here are very straightforward, like those for individual writers. For example, in cases where *both* literary form and period *are* specified *and there is no specific literary genre, subject matter, or audience*, the number will be the same as for a comparable individual writer except that it will have 08 (Collections) or 09 (Criticism) added to the end.

A notable addition is that the digit representing the literary form now includes 7 for Humorous treatment, which is not available for individual writers. Even here it can only be used if more than one literary form is involved; a collection of humorous plays is still plays, and would be classified in drama.

In other cases number-building is more complex than this. It is not feasible here to go through all the possibilities, but I will give some examples. You are advised to consult the flow charts in the Manual (Volume 1, pp. 31–2), because these have the advantage of forcing you to consider one question at a time, rather than panicking because you look at all the different aspects you are trying to specify. They are very helpful as a start, and in many cases will lead you to the complete number.

Examples

```
Restoration comedy (introd. Duncan Wu, 2002)
```

This is an anthology of Restoration comedies. Let's try following Flow chart B (Volume 1, p. 31) because this is the one for Works by or about more than one author. We shall go straight down the left-hand side of the chart, starting with 82, adding 2 for Drama, until we come to the question 'Specific kind, medium, scope?'. You might wonder what this means, and the best way to find out is to look at —2 in Table 3B and see the kinds of drama that are listed here. This *is* one of those kinds (Comedy), and so we complete the notation for that (—20523), making 822.0523 so far.

The next question in the flow chart asks whether the notation that we have just added is identified with an * asterisk. In this case (Comedy) the answer is Yes, and so we are told to 'Follow instructions in table under T3B —102–108'. This is the confusing part; it refers to the special table on p. 628 of Volume 1: —102–107 Specific kinds of poetry.

But, you say, we are not dealing with poetry, we are dealing with drama. The point is that poetry is used as the model for how additions can be made, so wherever it says poetry we should pretend (in this case) that it says drama. In the table we see that 08 means Collections of literary texts, which is what we have. We therefore add 08. But we have still not finished, because the instruction tells us to add notation 001–99 from Table 3C. Is this appropriate? We had better have a look.

When we look at Table 3C we find that 001–99 is actually the whole of the table; so we can add anything that appears in Table 3C. You may notice that —17 means Comedy. But we have already specified Comedy, and we do not want to do so again, so we ignore that. The aspect which we have not yet managed to specify is the period (Restoration), and we can do that using —01–09 Specific periods in Table 3C. At this point we have to turn back to the number for the literature itself (820) to find the appropriate period number. (Clearly, because every literature uses period notation in a different way, it is not possible to refer to this specifically in Table 3C, which is why the rather vague expression 'earliest period' is used in the example.)

The period number under 820 for Restoration is 4. This actually means 1625–1702, but Restoration is included in a 'Class here' note. Our final number is therefore 822.05230804.

Notice that the flow chart led us to specify Comedy *before* trying to specify the period. Ignoring the flow chart we should still find a similar instruction in Table 3B under —21–29 Drama of specific periods. If it were not for this instruction, we might have gone as far as 822.408 (anthologies of drama of the 1625–1702 period) and added further, ending up with Comedy specified at the end. The instruction is designed to prevent this from happening, and to make sure that the same combination of aspects cannot be specified in opposite ways.

American theatre book of monologues for men (ed. Stephanie Coen, 2003)

Again we are in Drama, this time American, so we start with 812. Flow chart B again leads us to consider whether there is a 'Specific kind, medium, scope', and we find Monologues at —2045. This gives us 812.045 so far. Again we see that there is an * asterisk against the heading, so that we can 'Add as instructed under —102–107'. We add 08 for Collections of literary texts, and turn to Table 3C to see whether anything is appropriate there. We have not yet specified that the monologues are for men, and this we can do by using section —9 of Table 3C. We see that Men is —9286 (this incidentally means either *for* or *by* men), so we add this to what we have already, making 812.045089286.

```
The Puffin book of five-minute bear stories
(illus. Steve Cox, 2003)
```

This is an interesting example. The stories are in English, and the fact that they are 'five-minute' stories means that we can start with 823.01, meaning Short stories (using —301 from Table 3B). There is a note saying 'Class short stories of specific kinds in —308'; should we take notice of this? If you look at the various specific kinds that are given in —308 you will see that none of these seems appropriate for bear stories. In other words, we are dealing *not* with a specific kind but just with a specific theme.

Seeing the * asterisk and following the usual instruction 'Add as instructed under –102–107' leads us to add 08 for Collections, which again takes us to Table 3C. Here we find that —3 means Arts and literature dealing with specific themes and subjects. This looks promising: can we find a number for bears? Yes, —362 means Animals, and we can go further: we can 'add to base number —362 the numbers following 59 in 592–599'. The number for bears in the latter section is 599.78, so we add 978 to what we have already, making 823.0108362978. You may think this is ridiculous, but it shows what is possible.

The book is clearly for children, and you may be wondering whether we should have specified that. It would be possible, but not at the same time as specifying the theme (bears). Look at the preference order on p. 29 of the Manual and read the accompanying sections; this makes it clear that the theme is more important than the audience. The flow charts should always help you to make the right choice.

```
The encyclopaedia of school stories (ed.
Rosemary Auchmuty and Joy Wotton, 2000)
```

Here we start with 823 because it concerns English fiction. Using Flow chart B again, we come to the customary question 'Specific kind, medium, scope?'. This time the answer is No: school is a theme, school stories are not a *type* of fiction in any of the senses listed at —3 in Table 3B. We therefore go to the next question across, 'Specific period?'. Again the answer is No. We are told to 'Add 00: then follow instructions in table under T3B —1–8'. The instructions meant are those on pp. 626–7 of Table 3B, under the heading

—1–8   Specific forms

So far we have got 823.00. This book is *about* school stories, rather than a collection of them, and so we go to 9 History, description, critical appraisal, making 823.009. We can go further, because the range 91–99 is used for specific themes and subjects, and we are again referred to Table 3C. Here under —355 Social themes we find —3557 Education, which is as close as we are likely to get; we therefore add this, giving 823.0093557.

Notice that in this case, because we are not specifying *either* a particular kind, medium, or scope, *or* period, we get two zeros immediately after the digit representing literary form.

You will notice in looking at the examples that quite often an important aspect of the subject is not specified until the end of the number. If we had a book of poems about bears, it would be quite impossible to classify it so that it came anywhere near the short stories about bears. This is particularly relevant when considering works written by or about particular groups of people, such as women. There is no way of bringing these together by giving priority to women in the classification.

900, 930–990 History

History occupies almost the whole of the main class 900. It starts with General (world) history at 900–909, which is unfortunately separated from the rest by the presence of 910 Geography and 920 Biography, genealogy, insignia.

The ancient world and Archaeology go in 930, the geographic division being the same as —3 in Table 2. For the modern world, you start with the base number 9, and add to it from Table 2. *You can be as specific as necessary by adding any number of digits*, even though the schedules only go as far as printing numbers for individual countries.

Each area or country then has its own set of period divisions. These are tailored to fit the events in that country's history, unlike the general ones which we have seen before, in Table 1. In most cases they are introduced by a 0, so that you can tell where the geographic element finishes and the period number starts. For the United States this is not necessary, because while 973 is used for the United States as a whole the individual states are designated by 974–979.

Look also at the instructions at the beginning of 930–990 and notice the special modifications to the standard subdivisions which are given there. All these have two zeros. These special subdivisions are used *only for the number for the country (or other area) without period divisions*; within an individual period you use the *normal* standard subdivisions as usual.

Examples

> Yesterday's countryside: country life as it really was (Valerie Porter, 2000)

Country life is one of those subjects which can be classified either in Sociology or in History, where you might not expect it. A work which was particularly sociological would go in 307.72, but general reminiscing treatment is normally classed in the number for the history of the country or region. In this case we start with 941 for Great Britain, and add (using double 0 because it is required) the special version of standard subdivision —09 as instructed at 930–990. The number for Rural regions in Table 2 is –1734, and we therefore add 009 + 734, making the completed number 941.009734. This kind of number is commoner than you might think.

> Wartime women: a Mass-Observation anthology, 1937-1945 (ed. Dorothy Sheridan, 2000)

This is another example that might be expected to be in Sociology, but here the emphasis is on the War, the contributions being by women. We therefore use the number for Great Britain during the Second World War, 941.084, and add the standard subdivision —082 to signify Women. Notice that because we have used a period division we add the standard subdivision in the *normal* way with its normal meaning. The final number is therefore 941.084082.

> Roman Chester: city of the eagles (David J. P. Mason, 2001)

The area number for Chester in the modern world is —42714; to make a number for Chester in ancient times you add to —36 the numbers that follow —42, making —362714. This makes the number for the ancient history of Chester 936.2714, but we are not quite there yet. We want to specify the Roman period, and so we look at 936.2, and find that the subdivision for the Roman period is 04. This can be applied not just at 936.2 but at any further extension of that number, provided that the 'approximating the whole' rule (see pp. 36–8) is followed. Chester is specified in Table 2, which means that we can add the period number, making the complete number 936.271404.

940–990 History of modern world, of extraterrestrial worlds

Pages 869–70 of Volume 3 give a special table of additional numbers that can be used at various places through this section, whenever a double dagger ‡ appears. Although it is not specifically so called, you can think of this as a 'wars table', because you will find that the instructions to apply it occur in relation to named wars. (Because it is a comparatively recent development there are several major wars, such as the two World Wars, where this table does not apply, because they had already been provided with a fuller division.)

Example

```
Air war in the Falklands, 1982 (Christopher
Chant, 2001)
```

The number for the Falklands War is 997.11024, and you will notice that this number has the double dagger ‡ next to it. This leads you back to the table, from which you can take 48 for Air operations, making the complete number 997.1102448.

Notice, incidentally, that with certain exceptions wars are generally classified according to where most of the fighting takes place, rather than according to which countries participate (see Manual p. 176).

910 Geography

Geography all fits into 910–919. The number 910 itself is used for general works, 913 for the ancient world, and the range 914–919 for the modern world. Number-building is straightforward to begin with: you start with the base number 91 and add to it from Table 2 for whatever you place you need to specify. Put a decimal point after the third digit, as usual.

Although only the three-digit numbers in the range 913–919 are printed, you can, as with History, add as many digits as you need to, using Table 2, to specify more local places.

You can then add further to these numbers if necessary, as follows:

- Standard subdivisions are introduced by 00; you do not use 009 because the whole of this section *means* Geography in the first place, and all geographic division is made by adding from Table 2 immediately after the 91.
- Then come various special divisions introduced by a single 0:

01	Prehistoric geography
02	The earth (Physical geography)
04	Travel
06	Facilities for travel[l]ers
09	Areas, regions, places in general

Of these, 04 is perhaps the most commonly used, as it is where guidebooks go. 06 Facilities for travellers is a new number introduced for DDC 22; previously hotel guides went with other works about hotels at 647.9. Both 04 and 06 can be further subdivided according to the period when the guide was written, by adding (without any 0 that may appear) notation from the appropriate area's or country's History schedules in 930–990. In the case of 06 you first add 1 before adding from the period notation.

Examples

```
Sicily (Sally O'Brien, 2002)
```

(I am assuming that it is apparent that this is a guidebook.) Here we start with 91, and add the area notation for Sicily, which is —458, making 914.58. We can then add 04 to specify guidebooks, and go to the main number 945 to find the period number: here we find that 945.0<u>93</u> is for the period 2000 onwards, so we can add the 93, producing 914.580493.

```
Budge's Egypt: a classic 19th-century travel
guide (E. A. Wallis Budge, 2001)
```

In this case we are dealing with a modern reprint of a guide originally published in 1890. Again we start with 91 and add the area notation for Egypt, producing 916.2. We can add 04 to specify guidebooks and then go to 962 to find an appropriate period division. The most suitable seems to be 962.04 which covers 1882–1922, making the final number 916.2044.

```
Recommended country inns & pubs of Britain 2004
(ed. Peter Stanley Williams, 2004)
```

This makes use of the new subdivision, 06, which we add to the number for Great Britain, to make 914.106. As in the case of 04, we have the facility to add further (in this case adding to 061) and specify the period by going to 941 and finding the appropriate number there. 941.086 is the number for Great Britain from 2000 onwards, and so we add 86 here, making 914.106186.

(Many libraries, of course, may decide not to add period numbers in these cases.)

It is worth noting that a wide variety of guidebooks to specific-looking subjects can go in the appropriate Geography number here + 04. These might include: castles, waterways, seaside towns, 'hidden' places, minor roads, walks, country villages, shopping guides, battlefield sites, curiosities, monuments, etc. You should not try to be too specific in classifying such material.

'Persons treatment'

This term perhaps seems strange at first sight. It is used instead of 'biography', because persons treatment can encompass other things than biography. Certainly it includes biography and autobiography, but many works concern a person in some way, or have a focus on a person, without really being biographical. In the case of art works, it often means works *by* an artist, or criticism of an artist.

Table 1 provides

- —092 for individual persons treatment
- —0922 for collective treatment (this can be further divided geographically)
- —0929 for 'persons treatment' of animals and plants.

The recommended procedure is simply to add —092 to the end of the number for the kind of person you are dealing with. If a person has been well known in more than one field it is sometimes difficult to know which subject to choose, but normally it is fairly straightforward. It is inevitable that if a person had a wide range of interests different books about the person will be classified differently because of differences in emphasis. And although in most cases we are recommended to be as specific as possible when classifying, in this case you should not take this to extremes. A cricketer, for example, will be classified in 796.358092, i.e. for cricket only, even if he is known primarily as a batsman, because it would not be helpful to go further. Further advice appears in the Manual, pp. 14–17.

Remember of course that the usual provisions about 'approximating the whole' (see pp. 36–8) apply.

Examples

> Irrepressible reformer: a biography of Melvil
> Dewey (Wayne A. Wiegand, 1996)

This is a good example of the problem of how specific to be. Dewey is now known primarily for his classification scheme, which has its own number, 025.43. Should we therefore class this at 025.43092? The book actually says very little about the classification, and it seems to me that it would be better to classify it with librarianship as a whole, at 020.92, because it covers his general contribution to the profession, and the rest of his life.

> Dictionary of legal biography, 1845-1945 (A. B.
> Schofield, 1998)

This is collective biography, which means that it goes in 340.0922 (two zeros required at 340). Table 1 —0922 allows us to add areas notation from Table 2 if required. In fact this book is entirely about British people, which means that we can add —41, making 340.092241. There is no way of specifying that it is a dictionary; you are allowed to add —03 after —0901–0905 or after —093–099, but not after —0922.

Here is an example of 'persons treatment' of an animal:

> The grey horse: the story of Desert Orchid
> (Richard Burridge, 2004)

Because Desert Orchid is (or was, until retirement) a steeplechaser, the number to use is 798.45, to which we can add —0929 for 'persons treatment', making 798.450929.

There are some exceptions where —092 is not used:

- in philosophy at 180–199

- in certain subjects in the fine arts
- in literature (see pp. 96–100)
- for collected persons treatment in 930–990 when no historical period is specified.

Individual philosophers

The philosophy numbers are rather unsatisfactory, because we are specifically forbidden to add —09 from Table 1. This means that not only can we not specify persons treatment, it is impossible to specify a particular period, or even, in the case of 193 which covers both Germany and Austria, to separate the two countries. Individual philosophers go in the country number without further subdivision, and no distinction is made between works by and about them. In practice you will find that most works classified here are by and about individuals rather than about the philosophy associated with the countries.

Examples

> The essential Locke (Paul Strathern, 2003)
>
> The Cambridge companion to Pascal (ed. Nicholas Hammond, 2003)

The first of these is texts *by* Locke, the second is *about* Pascal. They go in 192 (British) and 194 (French) respectively.

The fine arts

The way in which persons treatment is handled in the fine arts varies from subject to subject. In most cases there is no distinction between works by the artist and works about the artist, which has the useful effect of keeping them together:

- 709.2 is used for artists who are not known primarily for working in a particular field.
- 720.92 is used for architects.
- 730.92 for sculptors.
- 741 is unusual, in that, although persons treatment goes in 741.092, collections of drawings by individual artists go in 741.93–741.99, divided by nationality. There is the same distinction between 741.5092 and 741.593–741.599.

- 759 is also divided by nationality only, using the irregular areas notation described on pp. 65–7; you are forbidden to add —092.
- 760.092 is used for graphic artists.
- 769.92 for printmakers (760.92 does not exist).
- 770.92 for photographers, except that works consisting chiefly of actual photographs by individuals go in 779.092. This is further complicated by the fact that it is possible to specify the *subject* of the photographs before adding the —092, something that does not occur anywhere else.

Examples

> Barbara Hepworth centenary (ed. Chris Stephens, 2003)

It does not matter whether this is primarily biographical or largely illustrations of this famous sculptor's works: it will go in 730.92.

> Beaton in the sixties: the Cecil Beaton diaries as they were written (introd. Hugo Vickers, 2003)

Beaton was a famous photographer. This is not primarily a collection of his photographs, it is his diaries, which means that it goes in 770.92.

> Celebrity: the photographs of Terry O'Neill (introd. A. A. Gill, 2003)

In this case we have a collection of photographs of people, which means that we use 779.2; but we can still add —092 for persons treatment to this, making 779.2092.

Literature

As we have already seen (p. 96), works by or about an individual writer of literature go at the same number; you must *not* add —092 or anything else. The main problem arises when a writer is known for more than one literary form: which number do you then use for a general biography? The rule (see Manual, p. 26) is to use the number for the form with which the writer is chiefly identified. If there is no readily identifiable single form, use —8∪09 from Table 3 (see above, p. 99).

Examples

> Philip Larkin: a writer's life (Andrew Motion, 1993)

Despite writing in other forms, and despite being a librarian, Larkin is clearly best known as a poet and one would therefore expect a biography to go at 821.914.

> William Morris: a life for our time (Fiona McCarthy, 1994)

Morris's interests were so wide-ranging that it is difficult to choose an ideal number for him. He might go in 709.2, but if we want to classify him in Literature it will be best to use 828.809.

Collected persons treatment in 930–990

Collected persons treatment under the history of an area or country *when no historical period is specified* has a special form of the standard subdivision, —0099 (double 0 because all the standard subdivisions here have this), rather than the expected —(0)0922. This is not very often needed, but can be useful for collective biographies of kings and queens, or statesmen associated with a particular country.

Within a particular period you would use —0922 as normal.

Example

> British political leaders [electronic resource]: a biographical dictionary (ed. Keith Laybourn, 2001)

Although the word 'political' might lead us to think of the 320s it is usual to classify major political figures and statesmen with the country to which they belong. In this case, because no period is specified, we therefore use 941.0099.

Optional treatment of biography

There is the *option* of classifying all biography in 920–929, where a subject arrangement is provided. This is not the Editors' recommended treatment, however, partly because in the case of artists and writers it separates works about them from their works themselves. But bear in mind that many public libraries put all biography in a single sequence at 920, or unclassified.

If you do not use the option, you will still classify a few things in 920, but these will be only general collections and biographical dictionaries of the *Who's who* type, provided that they are *not* related to any particular subject.

Exercises

With the Law examples, try to give an answer using *each* of the options.

1 The mission to Ethiopia: an American Lutheran memoir (ed. Leonard Flachman and Merlyn Seitz, 2004)
2 A history of the Church of Ireland, 1691–2001, 2nd ed. (Alan Acheson, 2002)
3 A short history of the Liberal Party, 1900–2001, 6th ed. (Chris Cook, 2002)
4 Human rights in Australian law: principles, practice, and potential (ed. David Kinley, 1998)
5 An introduction to the law of health & safety at work in Scotland (Victor Craig and Kenneth Miller, 2000)
6 Unlocking numeracy: a guide for primary schools (ed. Valsa Koshy and Jean Murray, 2002)
7 Collins Gem French dictionary: French–English, English–French, 7th ed. (2003)
8 Better reading Spanish: a reader and guide to improving your understanding of written Spanish (Jean Yates, 2003)
9 Why teach mathematics?: a focus on general education (Hans Werner Heymann, 2003)
10 German dictionary of physics = Wörterbuch Physik englisch (ed. Ralph Sube, 2003)
11 Electricity and magnetism in biological systems (Donald Edmonds, 2001)
12 Introduced mammals of the world: their history, distribution, and influence (John L. Long, 2003)
13 Mouse phenotypes: a handbook of mutation analysis (Virginia E. Papaioannou and Richard R. Behringer, 2003)
14 Bat ecology (ed. Thomas H. Kunz and M. Brock Fenton, 2003)
15 Dolphin talk: whistles, clicks, and clapping jaws (Wendy Pfeffer, 2003)

16 Baby giraffe (photographs provided by San Diego Zoo, 2003)
17 Soay sheep: dynamics and selection in an island population (ed. Tim Clutton-Brock and Josephine Pemberton, 2003)
18 Sexual selection and reproductive competition in primates: new perspectives and directions (ed. Clara B. Jones, 2003)
19 Antimalarial chemotherapy: mechanisms of action, resistance, and new directions in drug discovery (ed. Philip J. Rosenthal, 2001)
20 Audiology: the fundamentals, 3rd ed. (Fred H. Bess and Larry E. Humes, 2003)
21 Does your child really need glasses?: a parent's complete guide to eyecare (Robert A. Clark, 2003)
22 Images of the dove (Jean Hansell, 2003)
23 Oil landscapes step by step (Wendon Blake, 2001)
24 Maritime painting of early Australia, 1788–1900 (Martin Terry, 1998)
25 Nature photography: learning from a master (photographs by Gilles Martin; text by Denis Boyard, 2003)
26 Mendelssohn's 'Italian' symphony (John Michael Cooper, 2003)
27 Total piano tutor: the ultimate guide to learning and mastering the piano (Terry Burrows, 2004)
28 Six carols for Christmas: for organ (arr. Robert J. Powell; ed. Dale Tucker, 2001)
29 Harmonium: the history of the reed organ and its makers (Arthur W. J. G. Ord-Hume, 1986)
30 How to play rock guitar: the basics & beyond, 2nd ed. (ed. Richard Johnston, 2003)
31 The many faces of movie comedy [videorecording] (iCommunication Center for Media Design, Department of Communications, Ball State University, 2003)
32 A short guide to writing about art, 7th ed. (Sylvan Barnet, 2003)
33 Four Renaissance comedies (ed. Robert Shaughnessy, 2004)
34 The alchemy of laughter: comedy in English fiction (Glen Cavaliero, 2000)
35 The Cambridge companion to crime fiction (ed. Martin Priestman, 2003)
36 Oscar Wilde [electronic resource]: the critical heritage (ed. Karl Beckson, 2003)
37 Finders keepers: selected prose, 1971–2001 (Seamus Heaney, 2002)
38 The unofficial guide to England (Stephen Brewer, 2003)

39 Let's go: Paris, 2004 (ed. Abigail K. Joseph, 2004)
40 The Peninsular War: a new history (Charles Esdaile, 2002)
41 Memorials of the Great War in Britain: the symbolism and politics of remembrance (Alex King, 1998)
42 Brave new city: Brighton & Hove past, present, future (Anthony Selden with Matthew Nurse, Edward Twohig and Chris Horlock, 2002)
43 The Boer War (Denis Judd & Keith Surridge, 2002)
44 Historical dictionary of Malawi, 3rd ed. (Owen J. M. Kalinga and Cynthia A. Crosby, 2001)

Persons treatment

45 Descartes's theory of mind (Desmond M. Clarke, 2003)
46 Runcie: on reflection (ed. Stephen Platten, 2002)
47 Cicely Saunders, founder of the hospice movement: selected letters 1959-1999 (ed. David Clark, 2002)
48 A dictionary of Japanese artists: painting, sculpture, ceramics, prints, lacquer (Laurance P. Roberts, 1976)
49 The complete etchings of Rembrandt: reproduced in original size (Rembrandt van Rijn, ed. Gary Schwartz, 1994)
50 Bernhard Fuchs: portrait photographs (with an essay by Timm Starl, 2003)
51 My story (David Beckham, 1999)
52 The History Today who's who in British history (ed. Juliet Gardiner, 2000)
53 Churchill (Roy Jenkins, 2001)
54 Adolf Hitler (David Taylor, 2001)
55 Napoleon (Paul Johnson, 2002)

9 Compound subjects

One of the difficulties of using any classification scheme is that the things you have to classify do not always fit neatly into the structure of the scheme as it exists. Many problems can arise, and it is beyond the scope of this book (probably any book) to give guidance on them all. Among the commonest problems, however, is that of works covering more than one subject, and the aim of this chapter is to offer some help with this.

We have seen that it is often possible to build a number that expresses various *aspects* of a subject:

- using —09 for historical and geographic treatment
- using —024 to show that it is written for a specific readership, or
- using —08 to indicate that the subject is treated in relation to a particular kind of person.

Another standard subdivision which I have not mentioned so far is —015, which allows you to add to —01<u>5</u> the whole of whatever follows 5 in <u>5</u>00–<u>5</u>90 to specify various scientific principles of a subject.

Example

        Microbiology of fruits and vegetables (ed. Susan
        S. Sumner, 2002)

This deals with the commercial processing of fruits and vegetables, which means that we start with 664.8. We can use standard subdivision —015 here (two 0s required in this case) to specify Microbiology from 579, giving 664.8001579.

These instances all show you ways in which different aspects of a work can be brought together and specified in the class-number. Often, however, a work deals with two or more topics that cannot be linked together in Dewey in any way. The problem is similar whether we mean the main subjects of the work or subordinate aspects; even treatment of a subject in two different geographic areas is not straightforward.

There are various ways in which more than one subject can occur in a work:

- One subject may be described as influencing or affecting another, e.g. the effect of advertising on purchasing, or the influence of Japan on Western art.
- There may be some other, less clear, relationship between one subject and another.
- A comparison may be being made between two subjects, or two aspects of a subject, e.g. between British and Japanese business methods.
- The work may simply cover two subjects jointly, such as drawing and painting, cats and dogs, Latin and Greek, or Greek and Roman history.

It is not always possible, or necessary, to distinguish between these different kinds of combination, and sometimes the presence of the word 'and' is the only indication that some kind of relationship between two subjects is involved.

Effect of one subject on another

When a work deals with the effect of one subject on another, the general rule in Dewey is that you use the number for the subject that is being *affected*, not the one which is causing the effect. Unless Dewey specifically provides a number for the combination, you are unlikely to be able to specify the other subject at all.

Examples

> Persian literary influence on English
> literature: with special reference to the
> nineteenth century, New ed. (Hasan Javadi, 2004)

Because this is a book on a subject that has influenced English literature it is classed with English literature. Although there are, as we have seen, many facilities for number-building in literature there is no way of specifying influence. The best we can do here, therefore, is to class it in a general number for English literary criticism, 820.9. This is rather unsatisfactory because it takes no account of an important aspect of the work.

> Japonisme: Japanese influence on French art,
> 1854–1910 (Gabriel P. Weisberg *et al.*, 1975)

Here again, the best we can do is use 709.44 for French art; we might perhaps add —09034 to represent the nineteenth century, but there is no way of specifying the Japanese influence.

Occasionally the rule about preferring the subject affected is reversed if it is felt more important to produce a different collocation of subjects. For example, 302.23 means 'Media (Means of communication)'. Here we find the following instruction:

> Class the effect of mass media on a specific subject other than
> social groups with the subject, e.g. effect on social change
> 303.4833, on a company's advertising policy 659.111 … [etc.]

Most of this is what we should expect; it is the words 'other than social groups' that are important. It means that all material concerning the effects on mass media on social groups, such as children, is brought together here, rather than being scattered through the numbers for the various kinds of social groups that might be affected. The specific social groups are catered for by the use of —08 from Table 1, which is printed in the schedules in order to give the instruction:

> Class here effect of mass media on specific groups, on social
> stratification

Example

```
The other parent: the inside story of the
media's effect on our children (James P. Steyer,
2002)
```

Because of the instruction, you start with 302.23, and add —083 from Table 1 to specify Young people, making 302.23083.

Sometimes a specific number *is* provided for the effects of one subject on another. This is comparatively rare and tends to be restricted to cases where the relationship is quite well appreciated and where there is sufficient literary warrant.

Examples

```
Arts & economics: analysis & cultural policy,
2nd ed. (Bruno S. Frey, 2003)
```

Some special numbers are provided for the effects of certain subjects on the Arts. One of these is 700.103, which is for Effects of social conditions and factors. Economics would be included here, as it is not feasible to express such a compound subject more precisely.

```
The molecular gaze: art in the genetic age
(Dorothy Nelkin and Suzanne Anker, 2003)
```

A similar range of numbers is provided in 701 for Fine arts in particular, using 700.101–700.108 as a model. In this case we can use 701.05, which covers Effects of science and technology.

Although strictly speaking these numbers are for *effects*, they tend to be used also for other vaguer relationships.

Relationships between subjects

These examples have led us on to cases where the relationship is less clear than cause and effect. Other sorts of relationship are equally difficult to specify, unless they are of the kind that may be expressed by standard subdivisions, or unless Dewey actually provides a ready-made number for the relationship. Again this occurs occasionally, where there is strong literary warrant.

Examples

```
Science and theology since Copernicus: the
search for understanding (Peter Barrett, 2003)
```

Here again we have a special number, 261 Social theology and inter-religious relations and attitudes, which provides some ways of specifying certain relationships. The numbers are largely ready made for you, and there is provision only for those topics for which there is literary warrant. The number required here is 261.55.

```
Muslims and the state in Britain, France, and
Germany (Joel S. Fetzer and J. Christopher
Soper, 2004)
```

322 provides a specific number for Relation of the state to organized groups and their members, and 322.1 is Religious organizations and groups. We can use —088 from Table 1 to indicate the particular religion, and then add 297 to represent Muslims. In this case, because three different countries are involved, it is not feasible to specify them, and so the complete number is 322.1088297.

```
Great Britain and the United States: special
relations since World War II (Robert M.
Hathaway, 1990)
```

International relations is another area where there is a clear need to be able to express relationships between countries, and the range 327.3–327.9 provides for this. Priority is given to the nation which is emphasized, so that in this case we start with 327.73, then add 0 and —41, making 327.73041.

Two subjects but one predominant

It is almost impossible to write about any subject without including at least some material about others. You should therefore always concentrate on the main subject of a work when classifying it. Sometimes however you find that although a work deals mainly with one subject the amount dealing with another is considerable. In this case you should still classify it according to the subject that receives the fuller treatment (Dewey introduction 5.7(B)). (You may of course be able to make an added entry for the other number in your catalogue, but you cannot shelve a physical item in more than one place.)

Two subjects treated equally

Some combinations of subjects occur frequently enough to deserve a number of their own. There are a few of these within 510 Mathematics.

Example

```
College algebra and trigonometry, 3rd ed. (Mark
Dugopolski, 2003)
```

Algebra and trigonometry is one such combination, and has the number 512.13.

There are other combinations of subjects, such as Drawing and painting, or Greek and Latin literature, which often occur in practice but are difficult to deal with in Dewey because there is no specific number for the combination. Nevertheless sometimes an instruction is given that the number for one of the subjects has to make do for the combination, e.g.

741 Drawing and drawings

Class comprehensive works on drawing and painting in 750; class comprehensive works on two-dimensional art in 760

or

480 Hellenic languages   Classical Greek

Class here comprehensive works on classical (Greek and Latin) languages

880 Literatures of Hellenic languages   Classical Greek literature

Class here comprehensive works of or on literatures of classical (Greek and Latin) languages

---

Examples

```
Comparative Greek and Latin syntax (R. W. Moore,
2000)
```

The number for Classical Greek syntax is formed by taking the base number 48 and adding to it —5 from Table 4, making 485. Because of the general instruction at 480 this will have to do for this book too.

```
Drawing & painting (Chris Dunn, 1995)
```

This combination is mentioned under 741, and again in a 'Class here' note at 750. Because it is a book of techniques we use 751.

These instructions are given because these combinations occur frequently. With other combinations, however, you are likely to find no instruction.

The general rule in these cases, unless a specific rule says something different, is that if the subjects are treated equally, you use *whichever number comes earliest in the Dewey schedules* (Dewey introduction 5.7(C)). This may seem rather strange, but it is simpler to have an arbitrary rule like this, and it is the only thing to be done in a scheme which does not allow you simply to add two numbers together to specify both.

Examples

```
Oxford/Cambridge: the applicant's guide to
Oxford and Cambridge (Liz Walker, 2000)
```

This is about higher education, 378, where geographic treatment in the modern world uses the range 378.4–378.9. In Table 2 the number for Oxford is —42564, while Cambridge is —42659; the former comes earlier in the table, and we therefore class this book at 378.42564. In this case the number chosen happens to represent the term named first in the title, but this is coincidental.

> Education, knowledge, and economic growth:
> France and Germany in the 19th and 20th
> centuries (Claude Diebolt, Vivien Guiraud and
> Marielle Monteils, 2003)

This deals with higher education for economics, and we therefore start with 330.0711. Table 1 tells us to add from the table to specify the geographic area. But we want to specify both —44 for France and —43 for Germany; what do we do? We have to choose —43 because that number comes first in Table 2, and the final number is therefore 330.071143.

(The result would be different if the work were *predominantly* about France; in that case we should choose —44.)

> The development of corporate governance in Japan
> and Britain (ed. Robert Fitzgerald and Etsuo
> Abe, 2003)

We can classify this in 658.4, which requires two zeros in its standard subdivisions. Japan is —52 in Table 2, whereas Britain is —41, and we therefore use —41 as it comes first, making 658.400941.

An exception is when the two subjects, when put together, constitute almost the whole of the next broader subject in the hierarchy; in this case you should put the work in the number for that broader subject.

Three or more subjects

If a work deals with three or more subjects, then unless one is clearly the main subject of work, you should put the work in the next number up in the hierachy that includes them all. In the Dewey introduction (5.7(D)) this is referred to as the 'rule of three'.

Example

> Building big [electronic resource]: bridges,
> domes, skyscrapers, dams, tunnels (WGBH
> Interactive Multimedia Group, 2000)

This deals with several different kinds of structure, of which bridges, domes and tunnels each have numbers in subdivisions of 624. Although this number does not technically contain the other two subjects 624 is the closest we can get to a number that includes them all, and so this is the one to use.

When all else fails

Something which can be useful if you are really stuck is to consider the possibilities one digit at a time, and never put 0 if you can put something more specific. By this I mean start with the first digit of the class-number, and ask yourself which main class the work falls into. Only if it is very general or covers several main classes would you put 0. Move through the rest of the number in the same way. (Something like this is referred to in the Dewey introduction (5.7(E)) as the 'rule of zero'.)

The same principle applies with adding standard subdivisions. They all start with 0 (except when you are told to add them in a non-standard way), and this indicates that *before* adding one you should be as specific as possible, i.e. by using a digit in the range 1–9 in preference.

Exercises

1 Common destiny: a comparative history of the Dutch, French, and German Social Democratic parties, 1945–1969 (Dietrich Orlow, 2000)
2 Comparing housing systems: housing performance and housing policy in the United States and Britain (Valerie Karn and Harold Wolman, 1992)
3 Road and rail transportation (Harriet Williams, 2004)
4 Verb clusters: a study of Hungarian, German and Dutch (ed. Katalin E. Kiss and Henk van Riensdijk, 2004)
5 Algebra and geometry (Alan Beardon, 2003)
6 Nuclear and radiochemistry: fundamentals and applications, 2nd ed. (Karl Heinrich Lieser, 2001)
7 Jaguars and leopards (Melissa S. Cole, 2002)
8 Greek and Roman technology [electronic resource]: a sourcebook: annotated translations of Greek and Latin texts and documents (John W. Humphrey, John P. Oleson and Andrew N. Sherwood, 2003)
9 Nutrient requirements of cats and dogs (National Research Council, 2003)
10 Architecture and the sciences: exchanging metaphors (Antoine Picon and Alessandra Ponte, editors, 2003)
11 Oxford & Cambridge (Blue guide) (Geoffrey Tyack, 2004)

10 WebDewey

WebDewey is available only via subcription, and you have to resubscribe annually, otherwise you lose access to it.

It contains everything which appears in the printed version, but with some additional features. Because it is electronic, you can search in ways which are not possible in the printed version, and it also includes a selection of Library of Congress Subject Headings (LCSH), which may be useful to you when you are classifying.

The main features are:

- You can search for words or numbers wherever they are appear, and you are not tied to using the printed index.
- If you wish, you can search in a specified index only.
- Searching includes Boolean operators, truncation and character masking.
- You can browse through the schedules, tables and index in the same way as in the printed edition.
- Having found an entry, you can browse up and down the hierarchy to see how the number relates to the rest of its class.
- You can move quickly to related entries, such as the Manual, simply by clicking on a link.
- The web version of the index includes many terms which are not found in the printed one.
- Selected LCSH are included for Dewey numbers.

What it does not do, unfortunately, is help you with automatic number-building. This is an area in which the capabilities of an electronic system ought to offer a vast improvement on the printed version, but as yet this potential has not been realized in any way.

Searching
As with most electronic information systems, there is a fundamental

difference between searching and browsing:

- Searching allows you to look for words wherever they occur.
- Browsing allows you to look for words at the *start* of their entries.

In either case, it helps if you are reasonably familiar with Dewey and with the terminology likely to be used. It is no good, for example, typing in something like 'French history' and expecting to be taken directly to the number for the history of France.

Searching is a very powerful tool because it allows you to choose from

- All Fields
- Dewey Numbers
- Captions
- LCSH (Editorially Mapped)
- LCSH
- Relative Index
- Notes
- All Dewey

and to combine terms using AND, OR and NOT operators. It is most useful when you have a very specific term which is likely to retrieve a relatively small number of results, or when you want to find something that is referred to only in a Note, or in the Manual, where it would otherwise not be indexed.

Browsing

If you choose Browse you can browse in

- Dewey Numbers (with Captions)
- Relative Index
- Relative Index (KWIC)
- LCSH
- LCSH (KWIC)
- LCSH (Editorially Mapped)

For browsing you have to know the beginning of the number or expression that you are trying to find. It is more like using the printed index, or like browsing through the schedules and tables themselves. You can, however, also use one of the KWIC (Key Word in Context) indexes, which index all words, not just the words at the beginning of the string.

In each case, of course, you need to make sure that you choose an appropriate index for what you are trying to do. There is no point in typing in a Dewey number when you have chosen the LCSH option, for example.

Tables

The simplest way to find a particular Dewey table is to use Search and type **t** and the table number you want, followed by two hyphens, e.g.

```
t1--
```

Library of Congress Subject Headings (LCSH)

When you are looking at a Dewey number you will sometimes notice at the bottom of the screen that there are some typical LCSH. These may be marked EM, PPT or SM, meaning:

- EM: editorially mapped
  This means that these headings have been manually selected by the editors as being appropriate for the Dewey number.
- PPT: *People, Places & Things*
  This is an OCLC publication listing over 50,000 popular LCSH with their corresponding Dewey numbers.
- SM statistically mapped
  These headings have been selected simply on a statistical basis, i.e. they are the headings that appear *most frequently* in association with the number given. You should not assume that they are automatically going to be the most suitable for the work you are classifying.

➤ Remember that the LCSH given in WebDewey are only very *selective*; you cannot get to a complete list of LCSH here. Also, only those marked EM have been revised for DDC 22; the others may refer only to older editions.

User notes

Much as you might write annotations on the pages of the printed edition, you can create 'user notes' in WebDewey. These enable you to make notes about your policy regarding using particular numbers, use of options, how difficulties have been resolved in the past, examples of built numbers, or for any other purpose.

If you have a site licence you can create either notes which apply across the whole institution, or personal notes. A single-user subscriber can create only personal notes.

Notes can be attached to any record, by clicking on the *Create* button. You then have to give the note a name, and type in some content.

Further information
Further information on how to use WebDewey can be found in the Web-Dewey User Guide at:
www.oclc.org/support/documentation/dewey/webdewey_userguide/

Exercises
You are welcome to try using WebDewey on the exercises in any of the preceding chapters.

Answers to exercises

Note: In showing number-building, when only part of a number has been added, that part is <u>underlined</u>.

Chapter 3
1 The internet (Mac Bride, 1999) 004.678
2 Library disaster planning and recovery handbook (ed. Camila Alire, 2000) 025.82
3 The Chambers encyclopedia (2001) 032
   This is a British encyclopedia, and so goes in 032. An American one would go in 031.
4 Philosophy: a very short introduction (Edward Craig, 2002) 100
   Notice that there is no way of indicating that this is an introduction.
5 Tarot: intermediate handbook (Trudy J. Ashplant, 2001) 133.32424
6 Psychology (Lewis Barker, 2002) 150
7 Stress management (Jeff Davidson, 2001) 155.9042
8 Introduction to logic (Harry J. Gensler, 2002) 160
9 Innocent civilians: the morality of killing in war (Colm McKeogh, 2002) 172.42
10 Charismatic glossolalia: an empirical–theological study (Mark J. Cartledge, 2002) 234.132
11 Understanding human communication (Ronald B. Adler and George Rodman, 2000) 302.2
12 Sociolinguistics: an introduction to language and society (Peter Trudgill, 2000) 306.44
   Notice that Sociolinguistics is one of the topics mentioned in a 'Class here' note under 306.44 Language.
13 Economics (Keith Brunskill, 2001) 330
14 Nuclear power (Ian Graham, 2001) 333.7924
   You might expect a topic like this to be somewhere in Science, but all kinds of energy appear in 333.79.

15 The plague makers: the secret world of biological warfare (Wendy Barnaby, 2000) 358.38

16 Modern nuclear chemistry (Walter Loveland and David Morrissey, 2003) 541.38
Again we have an example of a 'Class here' note for this topic under 541.38 Radiochemistry.

17 Electrical engineering: a concise reference (R. Kories and H. Schmidt-Walyter, 2003) 621.3
There is no way of indicating that this is a concise book.

18 Quiche & soufflé cookbook: a 2 in 1 cookbook that makes these French favorites easy, Rev. ed. (Paul Mayer, 1982) 641.82
Here we have an 'Including' note showing both quiches and soufflés under 641.82 Main dishes.

19 The handbook of human resource management (ed. Brian Towers, 2003) 658.3

20 Petfood technology (ed. Jennifer L. Kvamme and Timothy D. Phillips, 2003) 664.66
Another occurrence of a 'Class here' note.

21 Modern petroleum technology, 6th ed. (Institute of Petroleum, 2000) 665.5

22 Horse-drawn carriages & sleighs: elegant vehicles from New England and New Brunswick (Richard Wilbur and Peter Dickinson, 2003) 688.6
If you have found this, well done! 688 is a hotchpotch of all kinds of miscellaneous objects, including 688.6 Nonmotor land vehicles, which I am sure no one would expect to find here.

23 Art galleries of the world, New ed. (Helen Langdon, 2002) 708
Because this covers the whole world we do not need to worry about trying to specify a place.

24 Beginning origami (Steve and Megumi Biddle, 2001) 736.982
Again, no way of showing that this is a beginner's book.

25 The counterfeit coin story (Ken Peters, 2002) 737.4
Counterfeit coins are mentioned in a 'Class here' note under 737.4 Coins.

26 Painting with acrylics (Wendy Jelbert, 2000) 751.426

27 Juggling: from start to star (Dave, Dorothy and Ben Finnigan, 2002) 793.87

28 Extreme sports (Lee Linford, 2001) 796.046
Even this comparatively new subject has found its way into Dewey.

29 Geography (David Balderstone, 2002) 910
    There are of course all kinds of geography, but a general work would
    go here.
30 The essential guide to genealogy: the professional way to unlock your
    ancestral history (Ellen Galford, 2001) 929.1

Chapter 4

1 Extraordinary encounters: an encyclopedia of extraterrestrials and
   otherworldly beings (Jerome Clark, 2000) 001.94203
   This appears to deal chiefly with human–alien encounters, which are
   in a 'Class here' note under 001.942, which means that adding a standard subdivision is permissible.
2 The internet for physicians, 3rd ed. (Roger P. Smith, 2002)
   004.67802461
   Note here the use of —024 + 61 representing 6̲1̲0 Medicine; no final
   0 after a decimal point.
3 Libraries and librarianship in India (Jashu Patel and Krishan Kumar,
   2001) 020.954
   Because this covers libraries and librarianship it goes in 020. Beware
   of adding an extra 0.
4 Wise therapy: philosophy for counsellors (Tim LeBon, 2001) 102.415
   Another case of —024, but this time being added just to base number
   1 (of 1̲00) and therefore having a rather different appearance. The final
   15 represents 1̲5̲0 Psychology, which is what counsellors are involved
   in. If you have got this you have done very well.
5 Shropshire witchcraft (Charlotte S. Burne, 2002) 133.43094245
6 The HarperCollins concise guide to world religions: the A–Z encyclopedia of all the major religious traditions (Mircea Eliade and Ioan P.
   Couliano, 2000) 200.3
   A case of double zero in standard subdivisions, because the range
   201–209 has been used for other subjects.
7 Sweet singers of Wales: a story of Welsh hymns and their authors, with
   original translations (H. Elvet Lewis, 1994) 264.2309429
8 Dictionary of the social sciences (ed. Craig Calhoun, 2002) 300.3
   A similar case to the 200.3 example.
9 Encyclopedia of women in the Middle Ages (Jennifer Lawler, 2001)
   305.4090203
   305.4 = Women + (Table 1) —0902 = Middle Ages. The instruction

at —0901–0905 (top of Volume 1, p. 210) gives a list of further standard subdivisions which may be added, and this includes —03 Dictionaries, [etc.].

10 Economics for social workers: the application of economic theory to social policy and the human services (Michael Anthony Lewis and Karl Widerquist, 2001) 330.024362

Notice that 330 is one of the places where the normal standard subdivisions have an extra zero. 362 is added after —024 to represent social work.

11 Secondary breadwinners: Israeli women in the labour force (Vered Kraus, 2002) 331.4095694

This is a harder one. The nub of the subject is women workers, for which the number is 331.4. Adding to show Israel is then straightforward.

12 Career options for law school students (ed. Emily Dunn, 2001) 340.023

Another case where a double 0 is required for the standard subdivision. This is rather different from the other titles that have a 'for ...' expression in them. Clearly career options for law students must be in the Law or there is no point in writing a book specially for them, and 340 is therefore used as the starting-point.

13 Dictionary of military terms (Richard Bowyer, 1999) 355.003

Another example of double 0 in standard subdivisions.

14 Drugs in sport: the pressure to perform (British Medical Association, 2002) 362.29088796

This is a harder example. The interdisciplinary number for drug abuse is 362.29, and you want to specify that this is treated with respect to persons occupied in sport. This is therefore a case for —08, and you go to —088 for Occupational and religious groups. You add 796 because this is the number for Sport.

15 International dictionary of adult and continuing education, Rev. ed. (Peter Jarvis in association with A. L. Wilson, 2002) 374.003

Yet another example of double 0.

16 Art nouveau, New ed. (ed. Judith and Martin Miller, 2000) 709.0349

709 is based on 700 with —0901–0905 added from Table 1, but there are special extensions for specific styles.

17 Twentieth-century American art (Erika Doss, 2002) 709.730904

An example of adding —09 twice; first for place and then for period.

18 Manchester (Pevsner architectural guides) (Clare Hartwell, 2001) 720.942733

19 American architecture: an illustrated encyclopedia (Cyril M. Harris, 1998) 720.97303

Another example where —03 Dictionaries is added after first adding —09 + 73.

20 Aldershot's cinemas (Jim White, 1996) 725.82309422725

This is about the buildings, and so goes in 725.823.

21 Kenwood: paintings in the Iveagh Bequest (Julius Bryant, 2003) 750.7442142

This is quite difficult because 750 has some very irregular divisions. A note at 759 tells you to class exhibitions of paintings not limited by place, period or subject in 750.74. You might not assume that this also applies to collections, but it does, because —074 in Table 1 includes both exhibitions and collections. You therefore go to 750.74 and add from Table 2 as instructed at —074 in Table 1. Kenwood is in the London Borough of Camden, which is —42142.

22 The Penguin dictionary of music, 6th ed. (Arthur Jacobs, 1996) 780.3

23 Teaching geography in secondary schools: a reader (ed. Maggie Smith, 2002) 910.71241

It may be hard to see that 910.7 exists among the extensions to other standard subdivisions at 910, but it does. You therefore follow the instructions given at —07 in Table 2. It has 41 added from Table 2, because it deals with the United Kingdom, but you could not be expected to know this.

24 International handbook of underwater archaeology (ed. Carol V. Ruppé and Janet F. Barstad, 2001) 930.102804

930.1 Archaeology has a special development for Underwater archaeology at 930.1028, which is therefore printed in the schedules. There is no way of specifying 'international handbook'.

Chapter 5
Adding from tables

1 Psychotherapy and counseling with Asian American clients: a practical guide (George K. Hong and MaryAnna Domokos-Cheng Ham, 2001) 158.3 + (Table 2) 089 + (Table 5) 95 + 0 + (Table 2) 073 = 158.308995073

Note the instruction at the beginning of Table 5 about adding 0 and then from Table 2.

2 The Knights Templar in Britain (Evelyn Lord, 2002) 271.7913 + 0

+ (Table 2) 41 = 271.7913041

Follow 'Add as instructed' note in footnote.

3 Methodism in Crewe (O. E. King, 1997) 287.5 + (Table 2) 42712 = 287.542712

Because 287.5 means Methodist churches in British Isles, it is permissible only to add numbers relating to the British Isles at this point.

4 Gods and myths of ancient Egypt (Robert A. Armour, 2001) 299.31

This number is printed in the schedules, but is built according to the instructions under 299.1–299.4, using Table 5 —931 for Ancient Egyptians.

5 The identity and role of the German-speaking community in Namibia (ed. Hergen Junge, Gerhard Tötemeyer, Marianne Zappen-Thomson, 1993) 305.7 + (Table 6) 31 + 0 + (Table 2) 6881 = 305.73106881

In this case the instruction to add the 0 and then go to Table 2 comes from the schedules themselves.

6 Latin proverbs: wisdom from ancient to modern times (Waldo E. Sweet, 2002) 398.9 + (Table 6) 71 = 398.971

7 Foods of the Maya: a taste of the Yucatan (Nancy and Jeffrey Gerlach, 2002) 641.592 + (Table 5) 97 + (Table 6) 97_42_ = 641.5929742

Note the use of Tables 5 and 6 here.

8 Arabic typography: a comprehensive sourcebook (Huda Smitshuijzen AbiFares, 2001) 686.219 + (Table 6) 9_27_ = 686.21927

This means Arabic and Maltese, and is as close as we can get.

9 Early Celtic art (Paul Jacobsthal, 2003) 704.03 + (Table 5) 916 = 704.03916

10 Journey into the Arctic (Bryan and Cherry Alexander, 2003) 910.91 + (Table 2) 1_13_ = 910.9113

—113 in Table 2 means North frigid zone; there is no reference to the Arctic in the table itself, but if you look up Arctic in the index you are referred to this number.

Adding from elsewhere in (or the whole of) the schedules

11 Crystal therapy: an introductory guide to crystals for health and well-being (Stephanie and Tim Harrison, 2002) 133.25 + 5_48_ = 133.2548

12 Ethics and librarianship (Robert Hauptman, 2002) 174.9 + _020_ = 174.902

The final 0 is dropped from 020 as usual because it means nothing after the decimal point.

13 What the book [the Bible] says about sport (Stuart Weir, 2000) 220.8 + 796 = 220.8796

14 Women in science: career processes and outcomes (Yu Xie and Kimberlee A. Shauman, 2003) 305.43 + 500 = 305.435

You might have been tempted to try to put this in 331.4, but this book goes better in Sociology.

15 The European linen industry in historical perspective (ed. Brenda Collins and Philip Ollerenshaw, 2003) 338.47 + 67711 + 677.02864 + (Table 2) 094 = 338.476771164094

Quite a complicated one, and if you have got it exactly right you have done well. In this case 'linen fabrics' are mentioned in the number-building example under 677.112–677.117.

16 Food expenditures by U.S. households: looking ahead to 2020 (Noel Blisard, Jayachandr N. Variyam and John Cromartie, 2003) 339.48 + 664 + (Tables 1/2) 00973 + (Table 1) 01 = 339.486640097301

If you have got this, you have done very well indeed. Notice that in adding the final 01 you are following the instruction on p. 214 of Table 1, where 01 itself is the only part of —01 that can be added after 094–099.

17 Choosing students: higher education admissions tools for the 21st century (ed. Wayne J. Camara and Ernest W. Kimmel, 2004) 378.16 + 371.21 + (Tables 1/2) 0973 = 378.1610973

In taking numbers from 371.2 we could be more specific and specify procedures, but that is probably inappropriate here. You would not know that the book was about the United States, unless you guessed it from the authors' names.

18 More proficient motorcycling: mastering the ride (David L. Hough, 2003) 629.284 + 629.2275 = 629.28475

You might have expected motorcycling to be with motorcycles, but Driving is regarded as a separate subject, and is then subdivided by the type of vehicle.

19 The horse nutrition bible: the comprehensive guide to the feeding of your horse (Ruth Bishop, 2003) 636.1 + 636.0852 = 636.10852

20 Manual of bovine hoof care (J. Shearer and Sarel van Amstel, 2003) 636.2 + 636.089 + 617.585 = 636.20897585

A complicated one, involving adding part of the number for Feet.

21 Your outta control ferret: how to turn your frisky ferret into the perfect pet! (Bobbye Land, 2003) 636.9 + 599.76628 = 636.976628

Although this is specifically about behavioural problems you cannot add anything to show this, because the additional numbers shown under 636.1–636.8 can only be added when an * appears next to the number.

22 100 years of Harley-Davidson advertising (introd. Jack Supple, 2002) 659.19 + 629.2275 = 659.196292275

23 Coal – a complex natural resource: an overview of factors affecting coal quality and use in the United States (Stanley P. Schweinfurth, 2003) 662.6229 + (Table 2) 73 = 662.622973

24 Ferrous wire (ed. Allan B. Dove, 1990) 672 + 671.842 = 672.842
Although Wires are given at 671.842, in this case we need a number for ferrous wires, and therefore have to start with 672, which is divided in the same way.

25 Handbook of copper, brass & bronze extruded products (ed. Shirley Say, 1977) 673.3 + 671.84 = 673.384
673.3 Copper shows brass and bronze among the 'Class here' subjects. Again we add as in 671.

26 The golf club: 400 years of the good, the beautiful & the creative (Jeffery B. Ellis, 2003) 688.76 + 796.352 = 688.76352

27 Tennis stamps: the world of tennis in stamps, New ed. (2002) 769.564 + 704.949 + 796.342 = 769.5649796342

Adding from tables within the schedules

28 The HarperCollins study Bible. New Revised Standard Version, with the Apocryphal/Deuterocanonical books (ed. Wayne A. Meeks, 1993) 220.52043 + 4 = 220.520434
The final 4 is for Special editions, including 'study editions', from table under 220.5201–220.5209.

29 Canada's energy future: scenarios for supply and demand to 2025 (National Energy Board, 2003) 333.79 + 12 + (Tables 1/2) 0971 = 333.79120971
12 is for Requirements, from table under 333.7–333.9.

30 Reducing underage drinking: a collective responsibility (ed. Richard J. Bonnie and Mary Ellen O'Connell, 2003) 362.292 + 7 + (Table 1) 0835 + (Tables 1/2) 0973 = 362.292708350973
7 is for Measures to prevent ... [etc.], from table under 362–363. You were not to know that it dealt with the United States, of course. This final addition is permitted by the instruction at —08 (p. 202 of Volume 1), which

allows specific further additions.

31 A handbook of rice seedborne fungi (T. W. Mew and P. Gonzales, 2002) 633.18 + 9 + 632.4 = 633.1894

9 is Injuries, diseases, pests, from table under 633–635, with addition from 632.

32 Sue Cook's bumper cross stitch collection: 12 pictures and hundreds of motifs to celebrate the year (Sue Cook, 2003) 746.443 + 041 = 746.443041

041 is Patterns, from table under 746. This would be difficult to get without seeing the book.

Chapter 6

1 Manliness and its discontents: the Black middle class and the transformation of masculinity, 1900–1930 (Martin Summers, 2004) 305.3 + 305.48 + 305.8 + (Table 5) 896 + 073 + (Table 1) 009041 = 305.38896073009041

305.3 Men and women is above 305.5 Social classes and 305.8 Ethnic and national groups in table of preference at 305.

2 Thumbs up!: inclusion, rights and equality as experienced by youth with disabilities (Catherine Frazee, 2003) 305.908

305.908 Persons with disabilities ... [etc.] is above 305.2 Age groups in table of preference at 305.

3 Healthcare management dictionary (Annie Phillips, 2003) 362.1068

You cannot specify dictionary because there is no provision for adding further to —068 in Table 1.

4 Recommendations on the transport of dangerous goods: manual of tests and criteria, 4th ed. (United Nations, 2003) 363.17

363.17 Hazardous materials is above 363.12 Transportation hazards in table of preference at 363.1.

5 Occupational & residential exposure assessment for pesticides (Laire Franklin and John Worgan, 2003) 363.1792

This means Agricultural chemicals, with a 'Class here' note for pesticides. 363.17 Hazardous materials is above both 363.13 Domestic hazards and 363.11 Occupational hazards in table of preference at 363.1.

6 Food chains in a tide pool habitat (Isaac Nadeau, 2002) 577.699

577.699 means Seashore ecology, which comes later in the schedule than 577.16 Food chains. Instruction at 577 says to use the number coming last. Normally you could add from the earlier numbers (see pp. 84–6) to specify both aspects of the subject, but in this case tide pools are mentioned only in an 'Including' note under Seashore ecology, which means that number-building is not permitted.

7 The food chain (Under the sea series) (Lynn M. Stone, 2002) 577.7 + 577.16 = 577.716

In this case you again start with the number coming last, i.e. 577.7, but can then add from 577.16 to specify Food chains.

8 Small pet health care and breeding (Susan Fox, 2001) 636.0887

This is the number coming last in 636.08. Breeding is .082, Welfare .0832, but Pets .0887.

9 The diabetic gourmet cookbook: more than 200 healthy recipes from homestyle favorites to restaurant classics (Diabetic Gourmet Magazine, 2004) 641.56314

641.56314 Diabetic is above 641.514 Gourmet.

10 The low-carb barbecue book: over 200 recipes for the grill and picnic table (Dana Carpender, 2004) 641.56383

641.56383 Low carbohydrate is above 641.5784 Outdoor barbecuing.

11 IT auditing for financial institutions (Jimmy R. Sawyers, 2003) 657.83330453

IT auditing is 657.453 Auditing of computer-processing accounts, but table of preference at 657.1–657.9 gives priority to 657.8 Accounting for enterprises engaged in specific kinds of activities. We therefore go to 657.8333 first, but can then add from further back.

12 Getting a project done on time [electronic resource]: managing people, time, and results (Paul B. Williams, 1996) 658.4093

658.4093 Time management is above 658.404 Project management in table of preference at 658.401–658.409.

13 Canned cherries (pitted and unpitted) (Elizabeth Rodway in collaboration with the Canned Food Specification Club, 2003) 664.80423

664.804 + 634.23 for Cherries. You cannot specify preservation techniques because of instruction at 664.81–664.88.

14 Curve: the female nude now (Meghan Dailey, Jane Harris and Sarah Valdez, 2003) 704.9424

Here 704.9424 Female is higher in preference order than 704.9421 Nudes.

15 Crocheted lace: techniques, patterns, and projects (Pauline Turner, 2004) 746.22

746.22 Laces is above 746.434 Crocheting.

Chapter 7

1 Thinking through French philosophy: the being of the question (Leonard Lawlor, 2003) 194

2 Britain at the polls, 2001 (ed. Anthony King *et al.*, 2002) 324.941086

3 The French economy in the twentieth century (Jean-Pierre Dormois, 2003) 330.944081

4 American economic development since 1945: growth, decline, and rejuvenation (Samuel Rosenberg, 2003) 330.973092

5 The arts in the West since 1945 (Arthur Marwick, 2002) 700.9182109045

Because this is the Arts as a whole, use 700.9. You may not have got the correct area number for the West: —1821 in Table 2.

6 Becoming an art teacher (Jane K. Bates, 2000) 707.12

7 Up close: a guide to Manchester Art Gallery (Michael Howard, 2002) 708.2733

Notice that if the gallery were devoted to a specific subject, place or period it would not be classed in 708; you would have to use the number appropriate for the subject of the collection, and if possible add —074 from Table 1, then areas notation from Table 2. (Cf. exercise 10 below.)

8 The little book of the Louvre (Brigitte Govignon, 2001) 708.4361

9 Royal bronze statuary from ancient Egypt: with special attention to the kneeling pose (Marsha Hill, 2004) 732.8

If you expected this to go with other bronzes at 739.512 there is a reference there to 731–735 for bronze sculpture. Within that range Ancient Egyptian sculpture then has its own number. See also the Manual (Volume 1, p. 149).

10 Continuity and change: twentieth century sculpture in the Ashmolean Museum (Katharine Eustace, 2001) 735.2307442574

The sculpture is not restricted to a particular country, otherwise this would take precedence. To specify the museum we use —074 from Table 1, then areas notation from Table 2.

11 Painting in Boston: 1950–2000 (ed. Rachel Rosenfield Lafo, Nicholas Capasso and Jennifer Uhrhane, 2002) 759.144610904

This of course is Boston, Mass. 14461 represents 74461 from Table 2.

12 Ireland's painters, 1600–1940 (Anne Crookshank and the Knight of Glin, 2002) 759.2915

It is not impossible to add from Table 1 to specify period here, but because the period is so long it is not easy to find a suitable number, and so it seems better omitted.

13 Further studies in Islamic painting (Ernst J. Grube, 2003) 759.917671
A case where 759.9 introduces areas notation for the rest of the world not included in 759.1–759.8.

14 Australian painting, 1788–2000 (Bernard Smith and Terry Smith, 2001) 759.994

15 Dictionary of printmaking terms (Rosemary Simmons, 2002) 760.3
Notice that a dictionary of the graphic arts as a whole would be 760.03.

Chapter 8

1 The mission to Ethiopia: an American Lutheran memoir (ed. Leonard Flachman and Merlyn Seitz, 2004) 266 + 284.1 + (Table 2) 63 = 266.4163

2 A history of the Church of Ireland, 1691–2001, 2nd ed. (Alan Acheson, 2002) 283.415

3 A short history of the Liberal Party, 1900–2001, 6th ed. (Chris Cook, 2002) 324.241060904

4 Human rights in Australian law: principles, practice, and potential (ed. David Kinley, 1998) (standard number) 342.94085; (option A) 342.085; (option B) 349.40285; (option C) 342.85094

5 An introduction to the law of health & safety at work in Scotland (Victor Craig and Kenneth Miller, 2000) (standard number) 344.4110465; (option A) 344.0465; (option B) 344.1104465; (option C) 344.4650411

6 Unlocking numeracy: a guide for primary schools (ed. Valsa Koshy and Jean Murray, 2002) 372.720440941
Because this is about a subject in primary schools it goes in 372. Teaching is specified by adding 044 from table under 372.3–372.8. You could be excused for not doing this, and for not knowing that the book deals specifically with Britain.

7 Collins Gem French dictionary: French–English, English–French, 7th ed. (2003) 443.21

8 Better reading Spanish: a reader and guide to improving your understanding of written Spanish (Jean Yates, 2003) 46 + (Table 4) 864 + (Table 6) 21 = 468.6421

9 Why teach mathematics?: a focus on general education (Hans Werner Heymann, 2003) 510.71
This is not restricted to a special level, and therefore goes in the

number for the subject, with —071 from Table 1.

10 German dictionary of physics = Wörterbuch Physik englisch (ed. Ralph Sube, 2003) 530.03
The fact that this dictionary is German–English is irrelevant as it cannot be specified. 530 requires 00 for standard subdivisions.

11 Electricity and magnetism in biological systems (Donald Edmonds, 2001) 571.47
A simple example with no number-building required.

12 Introduced mammals of the world: their history, distribution, and influence (John L. Long, 2003) 599.162
Mammals are 599, and we add as instructed at 592–599. This gives 599.162 from 591.62 meaning nonnative animals.

13 Mouse phenotypes: a handbook of mutation analysis (Virginia E. Papaioannou and Richard R. Behringer, 2003) 599.35 + 591.35 = 599.35135
This number means Genetics of mice.

14 Bat ecology (ed. Thomas H. Kunz and M. Brock Fenton, 2003) 599.4 + 591.7 = 599.417

15 Dolphin talk: whistles, clicks, and clapping jaws (Wendy Pfeffer, 2003) 599.53 + 591.594 Acoustical communication = 599.531594

16 Baby giraffe (photographs provided by San Diego Zoo, 2003) 599.638 + 591.39 Young animals = 599.638139

17 Soay sheep: dynamics and selection in an island population (ed. Tim Clutton-Brock and Josephine Pemberton, 2003) 599.649 Sheep + 591.7 + 577.88 Population biology + (Tables 1/2) 094114 = 599.6491788094114

18 Sexual selection and reproductive competition in primates: new perspectives and directions (ed. Clara B. Jones, 2003) 599.8 + 591.562 = 599.81562

19 Antimalarial chemotherapy: mechanisms of action, resistance, and new directions in drug discovery (ed. Philip J. Rosenthal, 2001) 616.9362 + (from table under 616.1–616.9) 061 Drug therapy = 616.9362061

20 Audiology: the fundamentals, 3rd ed. (Fred H. Bess and Larry E. Humes, 2003) 617.8

21 Does your child really need glasses?: a parent's complete guide to eyecare (Robert A. Clark, 2003) 618.92097 + 617.7 Ophthalmology = 618.920977

22 Images of the dove (Jean Hansell, 2003) 704.9432 + 598.65 = 704.9432865

23 Oil landscapes step by step (Wendon Blake, 2001) 751.454 + 704.94<u>36</u>
   Landscapes = 751.45436
   You may have noticed that this is given as an example in the number-
   building intructions.

24 Maritime painting of early Australia, 1788–1900 (Martin Terry, 1998)
   758.20994
   We could perhaps also add from Table 1 —09034 for 19th century.

25 Nature photography: learning from a master (photographs by Gilles
   Martin; text by Denis Boyard, 2003) 778.93
   This is a book of techniques.

26 Mendelssohn's 'Italian' symphony (John Michael Cooper, 2003) 784.2
   Full orchestra + (from table under 784–788) 1 + 784.1<u>84</u> Symphonies
   = 784.2184

27 Total piano tutor: the ultimate guide to learning and mastering the
   piano (Terry Burrows, 2004)   786.2 Pianos + (from table under
   784–788) 1 + 784.1<u>93</u> Techniques = 786.2193

28 Six carols for Christmas: for organ (arr. Robert J. Powell; ed. Dale
   Tucker, 2001) 786.5 Organs + (from table under 784–788) 1 + 781.<u>723</u>
   Christmas day = 786.51723

29 Harmonium: the history of the reed organ and its makers (Arthur W.
   J. G. Ord-Hume, 1986) 786.55 Reed organs + (from table under
   784–788) 1 + 784.1<u>9</u> Instruments + (Table 1) 09 = 786.551909

30 How to play rock guitar: the basics & beyond, 2nd ed. (ed. Richard
   Johnston, 2003) 787.87 Guitars + (from table under 784–788) 1 +
   784.1<u>93</u> Techniques + (from instructions under 781.2–781.8) 1 +
   781.<u>66</u> Rock = 787.87193166
   A difficult example. Notice how the kind of music is specified *after* the
   techniques.

31 The many faces of movie comedy [videorecording] (iCommunication Center for Media Design, Department of Communications, Ball
   State University, 2003) 791.4361 + (Table 3C) —1<u>7</u> = 791.43617

32 A short guide to writing about art, 7th ed. (Sylvan Barnet, 2003)
   808.066 + <u>7</u>00 = 808.0667

33 Four Renaissance comedies (ed. Robert Shaughnessy, 2004) 82 +
   (Table 3B) 20523 Comedy + (from table on p. 628 of Table 3B) 08 +
   (Table 3C) 0 + (from 820, .3 being period number that covers Renais-
   sance) 3 = 822.05230803

34 The alchemy of laughter: comedy in English fiction (Glen Cavaliero,

2000) 82 + (Table 3B) 3 + 00 + (from table on p. 627 of Table 3B) 9 + (Table 3C) 17 Comedy = 823.00917

In this case, no specific *kind* of fiction and no period are specified, with result that we get 00.

35 The Cambridge companion to crime fiction (ed. Martin Priestman, 2003) 82 + (Table 3B) 30872 + (from table on p. 628 of Table 3B) 09 History, description, critical appraisal = 823.087209

36 Oscar Wilde [electronic resource]: the critical heritage (ed. Karl Beckson, 2003) 828.809

As this is a critical work of a writer who is known for various literary forms it is best to use (Table 3A) —8∪09.

37 Finders keepers: selected prose, 1971–2001 (Seamus Heaney, 2002) 828.91408

This is prose, which is —8∪08 in Table 3A.

38 The unofficial guide to England (Stephen Brewer, 2003) 914.20486 91 + (Table 2) 42 + (from table under 913–919) 04 Travel + 941.0<u>86</u> (942 has same divisions) 2000–.

39 Let's go: Paris, 2004 (ed. Abigail K. Joseph, 2004) 914.4360484 91 + (Table 2) 4436 Paris + 04 + 944.0<u>84</u> 2000–.

40 The Peninsular War: a new history (Charles Esdaile, 2002) 940.27 Peninsular War mentioned in a 'Class here' note.

41 Memorials of the Great War in Britain: the symbolism and politics of remembrance (Alex King, 1998) 940.4 + 940.5<u>465</u> Monuments and cemeteries + (Table 2) 41 = 940.46541

42 Brave new city: Brighton & Hove past, present, future (Anthony Selden with Matthew Nurse, Edward Twohig and Chris Horlock, 2002) 942.256

Because this covers past, present and future there is no point in trying to add anything to express period.

43 The Boer War (Denis Judd & Keith Surridge, 2002) 968.048

An example of a war being classified according to where the fighting took place, though with the option of classing it with British history instead.

44 Historical dictionary of Malawi, 3rd ed. (Owen J. M. Kalinga and Cynthia A. Crosby, 2001) 968.97003

No specific period, and so special modifications of standard subdivisions at 930–990 apply.

Persons treatment

45 Descartes's theory of mind (Desmond M. Clarke, 2003) 194

46 Runcie: on reflection (ed. Stephen Platten, 2002) 283.42092
Being Archbishop of Canterbury Robert Runcie is classified at the number for the Church of England.

47 Cicely Saunders, founder of the hospice movement: selected letters 1959–1999 (ed. David Clark, 2002) 362.1756092

48 A dictionary of Japanese artists: painting, sculpture, ceramics, prints, lacquer (Laurance P. Roberts, 1976) 709.2252
Notice that in collective persons treatment you can add further from Table 2 to specify the region. The difference between this number and 709.52 Japanese art is that this number implies that the book consists of individual biographical treatments of a range of artists, rather than being a more discursive general treatment. This is perhaps not a very useful practical distinction.

49 The complete etchings of Rembrandt: reproduced in original size (Rembrandt van Rijn, ed. Gary Schwartz, 1994) 769.92
Notice that there is a specific number for Etching (767.2) but this is only for the technique. Collections regardless of process go in 769.

50 Bernhard Fuchs: portrait photographs (with an essay by Timm Starl, 2003) 779.2092

51 My story (David Beckham, 1999) 796.334092

52 The History Today who's who in British history (ed. Juliet Gardiner, 2000) 941.0099
A case where no specific period is concerned, so the special modifications of standard subdivisions at 930–990 apply. This gives —0099 for collective persons treatment.

53 Churchill (Roy Jenkins, 2001) 941.082092
It can be difficult to find an appropriate historical period for statesmen. In this case 941.082 means the whole of 1901–1999, and although it is really too long it would be difficult to put Churchill into a narrower period.

54 Adolf Hitler (David Taylor, 2001) 943.086092
Hitler is particularly associated with the Third Reich, for which the number is 943.086.

55 Napoleon (Paul Johnson, 2002) 944.05092

Chapter 9

1   Common destiny: a comparative history of the Dutch, French, and German Social Democratic parties, 1945–1969 (Dietrich Orlow, 2000) 324.21 + 0<u>72</u> from table under 324.24–324.29 = 324.2172

For specific countries you would add areas notation to 324.2, but Europe, which includes the three countries mentioned, is not itself a country.

2   Comparing housing systems: housing performance and housing policy in the United States and Britain (Valerie Karn and Harold Wolman, 1992) 363.50941

—41 comes before —73 in Table 2.

3   Road and rail transportation (Harriet Williams, 2004) 388

388 is used for Ground transportation generally, although railways would go in 385. A case where the number for a general subject comes after most of the particular ones.

4   Verb clusters: a study of Hungarian, German and Dutch (ed. Katalin E. Kiss and Henk van Riensdijk, 2004) 415.6

There is no number which would embrace all three of these languages, and the best we can do is put it in the general linguistics number for verbs.

5   Algebra and geometry (Alan Beardon, 2003) 512.12

A case where there is a specific number for the combination.

6   Nuclear and radiochemistry: fundamentals and applications, 2nd ed. (Karl Heinrich Lieser, 2001) 541.38

This means Radiochemistry but has a 'Class here' note for nuclear chemistry.

7   Jaguars and leopards (Melissa S. Cole, 2002) 599.755

This number includes jaguars anyway, and leopard is subordinate to it at 599.7554.

8   Greek and Roman technology [electronic resource]: a sourcebook: annotated translations of Greek and Latin texts and documents (John W. Humphrey, John P. Oleson and Andrew N. Sherwood, 2003) 609.38

Roman is —37 and Greek —38, so that the normal rule would tell us to use —37 here; but there is a specific instruction at —38 telling us to use it for comprehensive works on Greece and the Roman empire. The same applies at 880, which is used for works covering both 870 and 880.

9   Nutrient requirements of cats and dogs (National Research Council, 2003) 636.7 + 636.<u>0852</u> applied nutrition = 636.70852

Dogs at 636.7 come before Cats at 636.8.

10 Architecture and the sciences: exchanging metaphors (Antoine Picon and Alessandra Ponte, editors, 2003) 720.105
Another number for a specific relationship.

11 Oxford & Cambridge (Blue guide) (Geoffrey Tyack, 2004) 914.25740486
Oxford at —42574 comes before Cambridge at —42659.

Bibliography

Comaromi, John Phillip (1976) *The Eighteen Editions of the Dewey Decimal Classification*, Albany, NY, Lake Placid Foundation, Forest Press Division.

Dewey, Melvil (1876) *A Classification and Subject Index for Cataloguing and Arranging the Books and Pamphlets of a Library*, Amherst, MA, M. Dewey. Reprinted: Albany, NY, Lake Placid Foundation, Forest Press Division, 1976.

People, Places & Things: a list of popular Library of Congress Subject Headings with Dewey numbers, Dublin, OH, Forest Press, 2001.

School Library Association website: www.sla.org.uk/

Wiegand, Wayne A. (1996) *Irrepressible Reformer: a biography of Melvil Dewey*, Chicago and London, American Library Association.

Wursten, Richard B. (ed.) (1990) *In Celebration of Revised 780: music in the Dewey Decimal Classification Edition 20*, MLT Technical Report, no. 19, Canton, MA, Music Library Association.

Index

References are to pages. Dewey numbers have not been indexed, but subjects receiving more than a passing mention in the text are included. A few references to notes in the answers to the exercises are also included.)(means 'compared with'.